THIS BOOK BELONGS TO:

....

THE BUMPER
BOOK OF NORWEGIAN
FOLK TALES

THE BUMPER BOOK OF
NORWEGIAN FOLK TALES

EDITED AND ILLUSTRATED BY HARALD NORDBERG

ASCHEHOUG

The Folk Tales are taken from
Peter Chr. Asbjørnsen og Jørgen Moe samlede eventyr 1. og 2.
© Gyldendal Norsk Forlag
© De norske Bokklubbene A/S 1982 and 1993

© 2001 H. Aschehoug & Co. (W. Nygaard), Oslo
http://www.aschehoug.no/

The book is published in collaboration with Dale of Norway

DALE OF NORWAY®
THE NAME THAT MADE NORWEGIAN SWEATERS WORLD FAMOUS
www.dale.no

Translation by Apropos Translatørbyrå AS,
Jenny E. Gillott and Kevin M.J. Quirk

Typeset by: Spektrum forlagtjenester
Paper: 115g Artic Volume
Printed in Denmark
Printed and bound by Aarhuus Stiftsbogtrykkerie, Århus 2001

ISBN 82-03-24425-4

CONTENTS

THE COCK AND
THE HEN IN THE
HAZELWOOD

Once upon a time a cock and a hen went into a hazelwood to pick nuts. And the hen got a nutshell stuck in her throat, and she lay there flapping her wings. The cock went to fetch water for her, and he ran off to the spring and said: "Dear spring, please give me water to give to Henny, my dear old hen, who is fighting for her life in the hazelwood."

11

But the spring answered: "You'll get no water from me until you bring me leaves."

And the cock ran off to the lindentree: "Dear lindentree, please give me leaves to give to the spring, who'll give me water to give to Henny, my dear old hen, who is fighting for her life in the hazelwood."

"You'll get no leaves until you bring me ribbons of red gold," replied the lindentree.

And the cock ran off to the Virgin Mary: "Dear Virgin Mary, please give me ribbons of red gold to give to the lindentree, who'll give me leaves to give to the spring, who'll give me water to give to Henny, my dear old hen, who is fighting for her life in the hazelwood."

"You'll get no ribbons of red gold from me until you bring me shoes," replied the Virgin Mary.

And the cock ran off to the shoemaker: "Dear shoemaker, please give me shoes to give to the Virgin Mary, who'll give me ribbons of red gold to give to the lindentree, who'll give me leaves to give to the spring, who will give me water to give to Henny, my dear old hen, who is fighting for her life in the hazelwood."

"You'll get no shoes from me until you bring me bristles," replied the shoemaker.

And the cock ran off to the sow: "Dear sow, please give me
bristles to give to the shoemaker, who'll give me shoes to give to
the Virgin Mary, who'll give me ribbons of red gold to give to

the lindentree, who'll give me leaves to give to the spring, who'll give me water to give to Henny, my dear old hen, who is fighting for her life in the hazelwood."

"You'll get no bristles from me until you bring me corn," replied the sow.

And the cock ran off to the thresher: "Dear thresher, please give me corn to give to the sow, who'll give me bristles to give to the shoemaker, who'll give me shoes to give to the Virgin Mary,

who'll give me ribbons of red gold to give to the lindentree, who'll give me leaves to give to the spring, who'll give me water to give to Henny, my dear old hen, who is fighting for her life in the hazelwood."

"You'll get no corn from me until you bring me a pancake," replied the sow.

And the cock ran off to the baking-woman: "Dear baking-woman, please give me a pancake to give to the thresher, who'll give me corn to give to the sow, who'll give me bristles to give to the shoemaker, who'll give me shoes to give to the Virgin Mary, who'll give me ribbons of red gold to give to the lindentree, who'll give me leaves to give to the spring, who'll give me water to give to Henny, my dear old hen, who is fighting for her life in the hazelwood."

"You'll get no pancake from me until you bring me wood,"
answered the baking-woman.

21

And the cock ran off to the woodcutter: "Dear woodcutter, please give me wood to give to the baking-woman who'll give me a pancake to give to the thresher, who'll give me corn to give to the sow, who'll give me bristles to give to the shoemaker, who'll give me shoes to give to the Virgin Mary, who'll give me ribbons of red gold to give to the lindentree, who'll give me

22

leaves to give to the spring, who'll give me water to give to Henny, my dear old hen, who is fighting for her life in the hazelwood."

"You'll get no wood from me until you bring me an axe," said the woodcutter.

And the cock ran off to the smith: "Dear smith, please give me an axe to give to the woodcutter, who'll give me some wood to give to the baking-woman, who'll give me a pancake to give to the thresher, who'll give me corn to give to the sow, who'll give me bristles to give to the shoemaker, who'll give me shoes to give to the Virgin Mary, who'll give me ribbons of red gold to give to the lindentree, who'll give me leaves to give to the

spring, who'll give me water to give to Henny, my dear old hen, who is fighting for her life in the hazelwood."

"You'll get no axe from me until you bring me charcoal," said the smith.

And the cock ran off to the charcoal burner: "Dear charcoal burner, please give me charcoal to give to the smith, who'll give me an axe to give to the woodcutter, who'll give me some wood to give to the baking-woman, who'll give me a pancake to give to the thresher, who'll give me corn to give to the sow, who'll give me bristles to give to the shoemaker, who'll give me shoes to give to the Virgin Mary, who'll give me ribbons of red gold to give to the lindentree, who'll give me leaves to give to the spring, who'll give me water to give to Henny, my dear old hen, who is fighting for her life in the hazelwood."

And the charcoal burner felt sorry for the cock and gave him some charcoal. And the smith got the charcoal, and the woodcutter an axe, and the baking-woman wood, and the

24

thresher a pancake, and the sow some corn, and the shoemaker bristles, and the Virgin Mary shoes, and the lindentree ribbons of red gold, and the spring some leaves, and the cock water which he gave to Henny, his dear old hen, who was fighting for her life in the hazelwood. And so she got well again.

WHY THE BEAR
HAS NO TAIL

Once upon a time the bear came upon the fox as he was prowling along with a number of fish he had stolen.

"Where did you get those from?" asked the bear.

"I've been out fishing, Mr. Bear!" replied the fox.

Now the bear wanted to learn to fish too and he asked the fox to tell him how.

"Why, that's a simple matter for you," answered the fox. "And it's easily learned. Just go out onto the ice, cut yourself a hole and hang your tail down through the ice. And then you need to leave it dangling there for a long time. Don't worry if it hurts a little, for that's when the fish bite. The longer you can keep it in the icy water, the more fish you'll catch. And then all you need to do, is to jerk them out of the water!"

Well, the bear did as the fox had told him and held his tail in the icy water for a long, long time until it got stuck in the frozen ice.

Then he pulled and he jerked and he jerked and he pulled –
until his tail snapped off short. And that is why the bear has no
tail, to this very day.

THE PANCAKE

Once upon a time there was a good housewife who had seven hungry children. One day she was busy frying pancakes for them. It was made of new milk, and it was lying in the pan, frizzling away, so beautiful and so thick. The children were standing around the fire, while the husband sat in the corner looking on.

"Oh, give me a bit of pancake, mother, I am so hungry!" said one child.

"Ah, do! Dear mother," said the second.

"Ah, do! Dear, good mother," said the third.

"Ah, do! Dear, good, kind mother," said the fourth.

"Ah, do! Dear, good, kind, nice mother," said the fifth.

"Ah, do! Dear, good, kind, nice, sweet mother," said the sixth.

"Ah, do! Dear, good, kind, nice, sweet, darling mother," said
the seventh. And thus they were all begging for pancakes, the

one more prettily than the other, because they were so hungry, and such good little children.

"Yes, children dear, wait a bit until it turns itself," she answered – she ought to have said "until I turn it" – "and then you shall all have pancake. Just look how thick and happy it lies there."

When the pancake heard this, it got frightened, and all of a sudden it turned itself and wanted to get out of the pan. But it fell down again on the other side, and when it had been fried a

little on that side too, it felt a little stronger in the back, jumped out on the floor, and rolled away like a wheel right through the door and down the road.

"Hey there!" The good wife ran after it, with the frying pan in one hand and the ladle in the other, as fast as she could, and the children behind her, while the husband came limping after, last of all.

"Hey there, won't you stop? Catch it! Stop it! Hey there!" they all screamed, the one louder than the other, trying to

catch it on the run. But the pancake rolled and rolled, and before long it was so far ahead that they couldn't see it, for the pancake was much smarter on its legs than any of them.

And when it had rolled for a while, it met a man.

"Good day, pancake!" said the man.

"Well met, Manny Panny," said the pancake.

43

"Dear pancake," said the man, "don't roll so fast, but wait a bit and let me eat you."

"I have run away from Goody Poody and her husband and seven squalling children, and I must run away from you too, Manny Panny," said the pancake, and rolled on and on, until it met a hen.

"Good day, pancake," said the hen.

"Good day, Henny Penny," said the pancake.

"My dear pancake, don't roll so fast, but wait a bit and let me eat you," said the hen.

"I have run away from Goody Poody and her husband and seven squalling children, and from Manny Panny, and I must run away from you too, Henny Penny," said the pancake, and rolled on like a wheel down the road.

Then it met a cock.

"Good day, pancake," said the cock.

"Good day, Cocky Locky," said the pancake.

"My dear pancake, don't roll so fast, but wait a bit and let me eat you," said the cock.

"I have run away from Goody Poody and her husband and seven squalling children, from Manny Panny, and Henny Penny, and I must run away from you too, Cocky Locky," said the pancake, and rolled and rolled on as fast as it could. When it had rolled a long time, it met a duck.

"Good day, pancake," said the duck.

"Good day, Ducky Lucky," said the pancake.

"My dear pancake, don't roll so fast, but wait a bit and let me eat you," said the duck.

"I have run away from Goody Poody and her husband and seven squalling children, from Manny Panny, and Henny Penny, and Cocky Locky, and I must run away from you too, Ducky Lucky," said the pancake, and with that it started rolling and rolling as fast as ever it could.

47

When it had rolled a long, long time, it met a goose.

"Good day, pancake," said the goose.

"Good day, Goosey Poosey," said the pancake.

"My dear pancake, don't roll so fast, but wait a bit and let me eat you," said the goose.

"I have run away from Goody Poody and her husband and seven squalling children, from Manny Panny, and Henny Penny, and Cocky Locky, and Ducky Lucky, and I must run away from you too, Goosey Poosey," said the pancake, and away it rolled.

So when it had rolled a long, very long time, it met a gander.

"Good day, pancake," said the gander.

"Good day, Gander Pander," said the pancake.

"My dear pancake, don't roll so fast, but wait a bit and let me eat you," said the gander.

"I have run away from Goody Poody and her husband and seven squalling children, from Manny Panny, and Henny Penny, and Cocky Locky, and Ducky Lucky, and Goosey Poosey, and I must run away from you too, Gander Pander,"

said the pancake, and rolled and rolled as fast as it could.

When it had rolled on a long, long time, it met a pig.

"Good day, pancake," said the pig.

"Good day, Piggy Wiggy," said the pancake, and began to roll on faster than ever.

"Now, wait a moment," said the pig. "You needn't be in such a hurry-scurry; we two can walk quietly together and keep each other company through the wood, because they say it isn't very safe there."

The pancake thought there might be something in that, and so they walked together through the wood; but when they had gone some distance, they came to a brook.

The pig was so fat it wasn't much trouble for him to swim across, but the pancake couldn't get over.

"Sit on my snout," said the pig, "and I will ferry you over."

The pancake did so.

"Oink, oink," grunted the pig, and swallowed the pancake in one gulp. And since the pancake couldn't get any farther, then we can't go on with this story any longer, either.

PER, PAUL AND ESPEN CINDERLAD

Once upon a time there was a man who had three sons, Per, Paul and Espen Cinderlad, but since the man was as poor as a church mouse, his three sons were all he had. So he told the three of them time and time again that they should go out into the world and earn their living, for if they stayed at home they would only starve.

A long way from his cottage was the king's manor, and right outside the king's windows an oak tree had sprung up. It was so enormous that it shut out the light from the king's Manor. The king had promised a great deal of money to anyone who could chop down the oak. But no one was able to, for no sooner had one piece been chopped off the trunk than two more grew in its place. The king also wanted a well dug to supply water throughout the year. Each of his neighbours had one, but the king had none, and he felt it a disgrace. To anyone who could dig a well to provide water throughout the year, the king had promised money and other riches. But no one could do it, as the king's farm was high up on a hill, and whenever they had dug a few inches down, they struck solid rock. Now the king made up his mind to have these tasks done, and he let it be proclaimed from the church doors throughout the land that whoever could fell the great oak beside the king's farm and dig him a well that provided water all year round would be given his daughter's hand in marriage and half his kingdom.

Now I can assure you that there was no lack of people willing to try their luck, but for all their chopping and hacking and all their burrowing and digging, they got no further. The oak tree grew bigger and fatter for every cut, and the rocky hillside didn't get any softer either.

After a while the three brothers wanted to set out and try their fortune. Their father was very pleased, for he thought that even if they did not win the princess and half the kingdom, they might find service in the household of a worthy man, and that was as much as he hoped for. And when the brothers made up their minds to go to the king's farm, their father gave his consent at once, and so it was that Per, Paul and Espen Cinderlad set off together.

After they had walked for a while, they came to a slope cove-red with spruce, and above it was a tall, steep hill. High up on the hill they could hear the sound of chopping.

"I wonder what's making that chopping sound on the hill up there?" said Espen Cinderlad.

"You're always such a wiseguy with all your wondering?" said Per and Paul. "It is surprising, isn't it, to hear a woodcutter at work on the hill?"

"I still think it would be fun to see what it is," said Espen Cinderlad, and off he went.

"Oh, if you're such a child, then it won't do you any harm to learn to walk as well!" his brothers shouted after him. But Espen didn't bother about them. Off he clambered up the hill, following the sound of chopping, until he found it came from an axe that was busy cutting the trunk of a pine-tree.

"Hello," said Espen Cinderlad, "I see you're busy chopping!"

"Yes, here I have been chopping a long, long time waiting for you," the axe replied.

"Well, here I am!" said Espen, and he took the axe and knocked off the handle and packed both the axe and the handle in his knapsack.

When he joined his brothers below, they teased him and laughed at him. "What was the strange thing up on the hill?" they said.

"Oh, it was only an axe we heard," said Espen.

After they had walked a little while further, they came to a rocky cliff where they could hear the sound of hammering and digging.

"I wonder what it is we can hear hammering and digging under that cliff up there?" said Espen Cinderlad.

"You're quite a wonderer, aren't you?" said Per and Paul again. "Haven't you ever heard woodpeckers hammering at trees before?"

"Yes, of course, but I still think it would be fun to see what it is," said Espen. And the more they laughed and poked fun at him, the less he cared. He climbed up to the cliff, and when he got there, he saw a pick hammering and digging.

"Hello," said Espen Cinderlad, "I see you're hammering and digging here all alone."

"Yes," said the pick. "I have been hammering and digging for a long, long time waiting for you."

"Well, here I am!" said Espen, and he took the pick and knocked off the handle and put it in his knapsack. Then he went down to join his brothers.

"What was the strange thing under the cliff?" asked Per and
Paul.

"Oh, nothing special. It was only a pick we heard," replied
Espen.

They went on for quite a while until they came to a stream.
By now they were all thirsty after walking such a long way, and
they lay down beside the brook to drink.

"I wonder where this water comes from?" said Espen
Cinderlad.

"If you're not crazy already, then all this wondering will make
you crazy soon enough!" said Per and Paul. "Where does the
brook come from? Haven't you ever seen water flowing from a
spring in the ground?"

"Yes, but I'd still like to see where it comes from," said Espen.

59

He hurried upstream, and even though his brothers shouted and laughed at him, he took no notice and walked on.

Much further up the hill the brook got smaller and smaller. Espen kept on following it until he saw a walnut out of which the water bubbled and babbled.

"Hello!" said Espen once more. "I see you're bubbling and babbling all alone."

"Yes, I do" said the walnut. "Here I have been bubbling and babbling for a long, long time waiting for you."

"Well, here I am!" said Espen. He took a piece of moss and pushed it into the hole to stop the flow of water, and then he put the walnut in his knapsack and went down again to join his brothers.

"And now you've seen where the water comes from. It must have been a strange sight?" Per and Paul jeered.

"It was just running out of a hole," said Espen. And the other two laughed and poked fun at him once again, but Espen didn't let them bother him. "Anyway, it was fun seeing it," he said.

They walked on for some time and arrived at the king's farm.

But since everyone in the kingdom had heard that they could win the princess and half the kingdom if they managed to chop down the mighty oak and dig a well for the king, and so many people had come to try their luck that the oak was twice as large as it had been to begin with. For you will remember that two new pieces grew for every one that was chopped off. Therefore the king had now decreed that whoever tried and could not fell the oak, should be banished to an island and have their ears chopped off.

But the two elder brothers were not afraid of what lay in store. They believed they would be able to chop down the oak. The eldest brother, Per, was the first to try his hand. But he shared the fate of all the others who had chopped on the oak: For every piece he cut off, two new ones grew instead, and the king's men seized him, cropped his ears and banished him to the island. Then Paul wanted to have a go, and the same thing happened to him. After he had chopped two or three times, the king's men saw that the oak grew, and they seized him too and put him on the island. And they cropped his ears even closer to his head, for they felt that he should have learned his lesson.

Then Espen Cinderlad wanted to try.

"If you really want to look like a marked sheep, we can crop your ears straight away, and save you further trouble," said the king, who was angry at the thought of Espen's elder brothers.

"I think I'd rather like to have a go first," said Espen, and they had to let him.

He took his axe from his knapsack and fixed on its handle again. "Chop and cut!" said Espen to the axe. And it chopped and cut so splinters flew, and in next to no time the oak was on the ground. After this Espen took his pick and attached the handle. "Dig and delve!" said Espen, and the pick hammered and dug, throwing up earth and stones,

and there was no stopping the sinking of the well this time. When it was deep and broad enough, Espen took out his walnut, placed it in a corner at the bottom, and pulled out the moss. "Bubble and babble!" said Espen, and the water came gushing out of the hole in the nut, and in no time at all the well was full to the brim.

And thus Espen had felled the oak which shut out the light from the king's windows and he also made a well for the king's palace. And in return he won the princess and half the kingdom, as the king had promised. As for Per and Paul, it was just as well that they had lost their ears, otherwise they would have heard everyone saying time and time again that Espen Cinderlad had not wondered in vain.

THE THREE BILLY GOATS GRUFF

Once upon a time three billy goats were on their way to the top of the mountain to get fat, and all three were called Billy Goat Gruff. On the way they had to cross a bridge over a waterfall, and under the bridge lived a huge, terrible troll with eyes as large as plates and a nose as long as a broomstick.

First came the youngest Billy Goat Gruff to cross the bridge.

Trip trap, trip trap, said the bridge.

"Who's that, tripping over my bridge?" roared the troll.

"Oh, it's only me, the littlest Billy Goat Gruff. I'm on my way up to the top of the mountain to get fat," said the billy goat in his tiny little voice.

"Now I'm coming to eat you", said the troll.

"Oh no. Don't eat me, I am so small. Wait a bit for the second Billy Goat Gruff, he is much bigger than I am."

"Well enough," said the troll.

Shortly after the second Billy Goat Gruff came to cross the bridge.

Trip trap, trip trap, trip trap, said the bridge.

"Who's that, tripping over my bridge?" roared the troll.

"Oh, it's only me, the second Billy Goat Gruff. I'm on my way to the top of the mountain to get fat," said the billy goat, in not so tiny a voice.

"Now I'm coming to eat you," said the troll.

"Oh no. Don't eat me. Wait a bit for the big Billy Goat Gruff, he is much, much bigger than I am."

"Oh, well enough," said the troll.

And sure enough, soon the big Billy Goat Gruff came along.

Trip trap, trip trap, trip trap, said the bridge, the big Billy Goat Gruff was so heavy that the bridge moaned and groaned beneath him!

"Who's that, tramping over my bridge?" roared the troll.

"It's the big Billy Goat Gruff," said the billy goat in a gruffy voice.

"Now I'm coming to eat you," roared the troll.

"Come on then! I have two long spears to poke your eyes out and your ears! And two big boulders to crush your bones and legs and shoulders!" said the billy goat. And with that he flew at the troll and poked his eyes out and crushed his bones to the marrow, and butted him into the waterfall, and went on his way up to the mountain top. Up there, the billy goats ate and grew fat, so fat that they were hardly able to walk back home again, and unless they have lost their fat, they are still fat.

Snip, snap, and don't you wail, but that's the end of the tale.

THE PRINCESS WHO ALWAYS HAD TO HAVE THE FINAL WORD

Once upon a time there was a king who had a daughter so stubborn and obstinate that she always had to have the final word. Therefore the king promised that anyone who could make her hold her tongue should win the princess and half the kingdom as well.

Plenty of people were willing to try, as you can imagine, for it's not every day one has the chance to win a king's daughter and half a kingdom. The gate to the king's manor didn't stand still for one moment; people came in droves, from east and from west, both riding and on foot. But no one was able to stop the princess talking.

At last the king let it be known that anyone who tried to silence the princess and failed, would be branded on both ears with the king's big branding iron – after all, he didn't want people rushing to his manor for nothing.

Now there were three brothers who had also heard talk of the princess, and since they were not too well off at home, they

wanted to go out and try their luck and see if they could win the king's daughter and half the kingdom. And since they got on pretty well, the three of them went together.

When they had gone part of the way, the youngest brother, who was called the Cinderlad, found a dead magpie.

"Look what I found! Look what I found!" he shouted.

"What have you found?" asked his brothers.

"I found a dead magpie," he said.

"Ugh! Drop it! What do you want to do with that?" said the two, who always thought they were the wisest.

"Oh, I've nothing better to do, and nothing better to carry, so I'll just take it along with me," said the Cinderlad.

When they had gone a bit further, the Cinderlad found an old willow hank, so he picked it up.

"Look what I found! Look what I found!" he shouted.

"What have you found now?" said his brothers.

"I found a willow hank," he replied.

"Pooh! What do you want with that? Drop it!" said the two.

"I've nothing better to do, and nothing better to carry, so I'll just take it along with me," said the Cinderlad.

When they had gone a little farther, he found a bit of a broken saucer. This he also picked up.

"Boys! Look what I found! Look what I found!" he said.

"Well, what have you found now?" asked the brothers.

"A bit of a broken saucer," he said.

"Ugh! Now that was something to take along! Drop it!" they said.

"Oh, I've nothing better to do, and nothing better to carry, so I'll just take it along with me," replied the Cinderlad.

When they had gone a little further, he found a crooked ram's horn, and just after he found the mate to it.

"Look what I found! Look what I found, boys!" he shouted.

"What have you found now?" said the others.

"Two ram's horns," answered the Cinderlad.

"Ugh! Drop them. What are you going to do with them?" they said.

"Oh, I've nothing better to do, and nothing better to carry, so I'll just take them along with me," said the Cinderlad.

In a little while he found a wedge.

"Hey, guys! Look what I found! Look what I found!" he shouted.

"That's a mighty lot of finding you've been doing! What have you found this time?" said the two eldest.

"I found a wedge," he replied.

"Oh, drop it! What are you going to do with that?" they said.

"I've nothing better to do, and nothing better to carry, so I'll just take it along with me," said the Cinderlad.

As they walked over the fields by the king's manor – where manure had recently been spread – the Cinderlad bent down and picked up a worn-out shoe sole.

"Say, fellows! Look what I found! Look what I found!" he said.

"If only you'd find a little sense by the time you got there!" said the two. "What did you find this time?"

"A worn-out shoe sole," he replied.

"Ugh! That was really something to pick up! Drop it! What are you going to do with it?" said the brothers.

"Oh, I've nothing better to do, and nothing better to carry, so I'll just take it along with me, if I'm to win the princess and half the kingdom," said the Cinderlad.

"Yes, you're likely to do that, you are!" said the two.

Then they were let in to the princess – first the eldest.

"Good day!" he said. "Good day, yourself!" she said, twisting and turning.

"It's terribly warm in here," he said.

"It's warmer in the coals," replied the princess.

There lay the branding iron, ready and waiting. When he saw this, his courage failed him right away, and so it was all up with him.

The middle brother didn't fare any better.

"Good day!" he said.

"Good day, yourself!" she said, starting to squirm.

"It's terribly hot in here," he said.

"It's hotter in the coals," she said. At that, he too lost both voice and speech, and so it was out with the iron again.

Then came the Cinderlad.

"Good day!" he said.

"Good day, yourself," she replied, twisting and turning.

"It's good and warm in here," said the Cinderlad.

"It's warmer in the coals," she replied. A third one didn't make her temper any sweeter.

"I suppose I can roast my magpie there, then?" he asked.

"I'm afraid she'll burst," said the king's daughter.

"Oh, that's no trouble! I'll put this willow hank around it," replied the boy.

"It's too wide!" she said.

"I'll drive in a wedge!" said the boy, and took out the wedge.

"The fat will run off her!" said the king's daughter.

"I'll catch it in this!" replied the boy, and held up the bit of broken saucer.

"You're twisting my words!" said the princess.

"No! Your words aren't twisted, but this is!" replied the boy, and took out one of the ram's horns.

"Well! I've never seen the like!" shouted the princess.

"Here's the like of it!" said the boy, and took out the other one.

"You're bent on wearing me out, aren't you?" she said.

"No, you're not worn-out, but this is!" replied the boy, and pulled out the shoe sole.

So the princess had to hold her tongue!

"Now, you're mine!" said the Cinderlad, and so he got her, and half the realm and kingdom into the bargain.

THE PIG
AND HIS
WAY OF LIFE

Once upon a time there was a pig who was fed up with his way of life. One day he decided to go to the courthouse and get a verdict on his mode of living. He wanted to try his luck like anyone else. Either way things could only get better.

"What is your complaint?" asked the court recorder.

"I'm so unhappy with my way of life," said the pig. "The horse gets oats, the cow gets grain. And they even get to rest in

nice, dry stalls. All I get is swill and leftovers. During the day I wallow in mud, while at night I lie in dirt and wet hay. I ask you, is there any justice in that?"

"No," answered the court recorder, "I do believe you have cause for complaint." He studied his law books and then passed judgment: "It is unjust that you should fare so badly," he said. "From this day on you shall eat peas and wheat, and sleep on a bed of silk."

The pig thanked the court recorder and was so happy that he didn't even notice whether it was day or night. On the way

home he grunted happily, mumbling to himself: "Peas and wheat, peas and wheat! Sleep on a beautiful, silken sheet! Peas and wheat, peas and wheat! Sleep on a beautiful, silken sheet!"

The road passed through a forest. Behind some bushes along the roadside lay a fox listening. As always, the fox was up to no good, and he decided to play a trick on the pig. In a fine and gentle voice the fox began to chant: "Rubbish and more, rubbish and more! Sleep on filthy, dirty straw!"

To begin with the pig didn't pay any attention to the fox; instead he carried on mumbling to himself: "Peas and wheat, peas and wheat! Sleep on a beautiful, silken sheet!" But the fox continued too: "Rubbish and more, rubbish and more! Sleep on filthy, dirty straw!" Slowly but surely, the words sank into the brain of the pig, and he began to repeat the words of the fox.

When the pig came home, everybody wanted to know the outcome of the court hearing: "Did they reach a decision to improve your way of life?" they asked.

"Yes, indeed!" replied the pig. "Well, what did they say?" they asked. "Rubbish and more, rubbish and more! Sleep on filthy, dirty straw!"

LITTLE AASE
GOOSEGIRL

Once upon a time there was a king who had so many geese
that he had to hire a girl just to watch them. Her name was
Aase, and so they called her Aase Goosegirl.

Now, at this time a prince of England was travelling around
the kingdom looking for a wife, and Aase sat herself down in
his path.

"Do you sit there, little Aase?" said the prince.

"Yes, I sit here sewing patch on to patch and darning all my
darned holes, for I'm expecting the prince of England today,"
said little Aase.

"Well, you can't expect to have him," said the prince.

"Oh yes, if it's him I shall have, then it's him I shall get," said little Aase.

Painters were sent to every country and every kingdom to paint the portraits of all the fairest princesses. The prince would then choose between them. He liked one of them so much that he travelled to her home and asked her to marry him, and he was overjoyed when she accepted to be his sweetheart. But the prince had brought with him a stone that he put in front of his bed, and this stone knew all things, and when the princess came, Little Aase Goosegirl said to her that if she had had a sweetheart before, or if she had any secrets that she didn't want the prince to know, she must not step over the stone he had in front of his bed.

"For it will tell him everything about you," she said.
When the princess heard this, she grew very sad, as you can imagine. But then she had the idea of asking Aase to go to the prince instead of her at night, and once he had fallen asleep, they would swap places again, so that he would have the right one next to him when the morning came.

And so they did.

When Little Aase Goosegirl came and trod on the stone, the prince asked: "Who is climbing into my bed?"

"A maiden pure and good!" said the stone, and they went to sleep. But during the night, the princess came into bed instead of Aase.

In the morning, when it was time to get up, the prince asked the stone again: "Who is climbing out of my bed?"

"Someone who has had three lovers," said the stone.

When the prince heard this, he didn't want to marry her, that much is sure. And so he sent her home again and found himself a new sweetheart to take her place.

While he was on his way to visit her, Little Aase Goosegirl had again sat down in his way.

"Do you sit there, Little Aase Goosegirl" said the prince.

"Yes, I sit here sewing patch on to patch and darning all my darned holes, for I'm expecting the prince of England today," said Aase.

"Well, you can't expect to have him," said the prince.

"Oh yes I can, if it's him I shall have, then it's him I shall get," said little Aase.

The same fate befell this princess as the first one, except that when she got up in the morning, the stone said that *she* had had six lovers. So the prince didn't want to marry her either and chased her off. But still he wanted to try to find a maiden who was pure and good. Again he searched far and wide in many countries until he found a girl he liked.

But as he was on his way to visit her, he passed Little Aase Goosegirl, who had again sat down in his way.

"Do you sit there, Little Aase Goosegirl?" said the prince.

"Yes, I sit here sewing patch on to patch and darning all my darned holes, for I'm expecting the prince of England today," said little Aase.

"Well, you can't expect to have him," said the prince.

"Oh yes I can, if it's him that I shall have, then it's him I shall get," said little Aase.

When the princess came, Little Aase Goosegirl said to her, as she had said to the other two, that if she had had any sweethearts before or had any other secrets that she didn't want the prince to find out, she must not tread on the stone that the prince had in front of his bed.

"For it tells him everything," she said.
The princess was upset when she heard this, but she was as cunning as the other two and asked Aase if she would go to bed with the prince at night instead of her. Once he had fallen asleep, they would swap places again, so that he had the right one next to him when the morning came.

And so they did.

When Little Aase Goosegirl came and trod on the stone, the prince asked: "Who is climbing into my bed?"

"A maiden pure and good!" said the stone, and so they lay down to sleep.

In the middle of the night, the prince slipped a ring on to Aase's finger, and it was so tight she could not get it off again.

For the prince could well understand something was going on, and he wanted a way of recognizing who was the right one. When the prince had fallen asleep, the princess came and chased Aase down to the goose pen and lay down in her place.

In the morning, when it was time to get up, the prince asked the stone again: "Who is climbing out of my bed?"

"Someone who has had nine lovers," said the stone, and when the prince heard this, he became so angry that he chased her off right there and then. Then he asked the stone what had happened with all these princesses who had stepped on the stone, for he could not understand it, he said. The stone ex-

plained how it had happened that they had fooled him and
sent Little Aase Goosegirl in their place. The prince wanted to
find out if this was so, so he went down to where she sat
watching the geese to see if she was wearing his ring. If she
has it, then it will be best to take her as my queen, he thought.
When he arrived at the place where she sat, he saw at once
that she had tied a piece of cloth around one of her fingers,
and he asked her why she had done that.

"Oh, I cut myself so badly," said Little Aase Goosegirl.
The prince wanted to take a closer look at her finger, but Aase
did not want to remove the piece of cloth. The prince grabbed
her finger, but Aase struggled and pulled her hand back again.
Then the cloth fell off, and the prince recognized his ring. So

he took her back to the palace with him and dressed her up in
all sorts of finery and beautiful clothes, and then they got married. And in this way Little Aase Goosegirl got the prince of
England after all – because it was him she should have.

THE SEVENTH
FATHER OF THE
HOUSE

Once upon a time there was a man who was out
travelling. At long last he came to a beautiful, big farm
with a manor house so fine that it could just as well have been
a small castle.

"This will be a good place to rest," he said to himself as he went in through the gate. An old man, with grey hair and a beard, was chopping wood nearby.

"Good evening, father," said the traveller. "Can you put me up for the night?"

"I'm not the father of the house," said the old man. "Go into the kitchen and talk to my father."

The traveller went into the kitchen, where he found a man who was even older, kneeling down in front of the hearth, blowing on the fire.

"Good evening, father. Could you put me up for the night?" asked the traveller.

"I'm not the father of the house," said the old fellow. "Go in and speak to my father. He's sitting by the table in the living room."

So the traveller went into the living room and spoke with the man who was sitting by the table. He was much older than both the others, and he sat, shivering and shaking, his teeth chattering, reading from a big book almost like a little child.

"Good evening, father. Will you put me up for the night?" said the man.

"I'm not the father of the house, but talk to my father, who's sitting on the bench," said the old man who sat by the table, shivering and shaking, his teeth chattering.

So the traveller went over to the man who was sitting on the

bench, and he was trying to smoke a pipe of tobacco. But he was so huddled up, and his hands were shaking so badly that he could hardly hold onto the pipe.

"Good evening, father," said the traveller again. "Can you put me up for the night?"

"I'm not the father of the house," replied the huddled-up old man. "But talk to my father who is lying in the bed."

So the traveller went over to the bed. And there on the bed lay an old, old man in whom there was no sign of life but a pair of big eyes.

"Good evening, father. Can you put me up for the night?" said the traveller.

"I'm not the father of the house, but talk to my father who's lying in the cradle," said the man with the big eyes.

Well, the traveller went over to the cradle. There lay an ancient man, so shrivelled and wrinkled that he was no bigger than a baby. And there was no way to tell whether there was life in him except for a rattle in his throat now and then.

"Good evening, father. Can you put me up for the night?" asked the man.

A long time passed before he got an answer, and it took even longer before the old man finished replying. He said – like all the others – that he was not the father of the house. "But talk to my father. He's hanging in the horn on the wall."

The traveller peered up along the walls, and at last he did catch sight of the horn. But when he tried to see who was lying in it, all he could see was a little ashen form that looked like a human face.

Now he was so frightened that he shouted out: "Good evening, father! Will you put me up for the night?"

A squeaking sound like that made by a tiny titmouse came from the horn, and it was all the traveller could do to understand what the sound meant: "Yes, my child."

And then in came a table laid with the costliest dishes, and with beer and spirits, too. And when the traveller had finished eating and drinking, in came a bed covered with reindeer hides. And he was very glad that at long last he had found the true father of the house.

LITTLE THUMB

Once upon a time there was a woman who had only one son, and he was no taller than your thumb. So they called him Little Thumb.

One day, when he was old enough to look after himself, his mother told him to go out and find himself a wife, as she meant it was about time he thought about getting married. When Little Thumb heard this, he was very happy. Once they had fixed up the cart, they set off, and his mother sat him on her lap. They were going to a manor, where there was a really big princess, but when they had travelled only a little of the way, Little Thumb was suddenly gone. The woman looked everywhere for him, and wept because he was lost and she couldn't find him.

"Yoo-hoo!" called Little Thumb, for he had hidden in the horse's mane. He jumped out and promised not to do it again. When they had driven a little further, Little Thumb was suddenly gone again. His mother looked for him and called for him and wept, but he was lost.

"Yoo-hoo!" called Little Thumb. She could hear him laughing and tittering, but she couldn't find him anywhere.

"Yoo-hoo, I'm over here!" said Little Thumb and jumped out from the horse's ear. His mother made him promise he wouldn't hide again. But when they had driven on a little further, he was suddenly gone again; he simply couldn't help himself. His mother looked for him and wept and called for him, but he was well and truly lost, and though she looked, she couldn't find him anywhere.

"Yoo-hoo, here I am!" called Little Thumb. But his mother just couldn't work out where he might be, for his voice sounded muffled. She looked high and low for him, while he kept on calling out "Yoo-hoo, here I am!" and laughing and gloating

because she couldn't find him. Then, all of a sudden, the horse sneezed, and sneezed out Little Thumb, for he had been hiding in one of its nostrils. This time his mother grabbed him and put him in a bag. She didn't know what else to do, as she understood he couldn't grow out of kind.

When they arrived at the manor, the couple was soon engaged to be married, because the big princess thought he was a handsome little boy, and it wasn't long before they were wed.

When it was time for the wedding feast in the manor, Little Thumb sat next to the princess at the table. But he was worse than badly off, for when he tried to eat, he couldn't reach the food, and he probably wouldn't have had a bite if the princess had not helped him up on to the table. Everything was fine as long as he could eat from the plate, but then they brought in a huge bowl of porridge. He couldn't reach over the rim, but Little Thumb found a way out; he jumped up and balanced on the edge of the bowl. Right in the middle of the bowl was a golden pool of melted butter, but he couldn't reach it from the edge of the bowl, so he sat down at the edge of the pool of

butter. Just then, the princess reached over with a huge spoonful of porridge to dip in the butter, but she came too close to Little Thumb and knocked him into the melted butter, and he was drowned.

THE MAN WHO KEPT HOUSE

Once upon a time there was a grumpy and bad-tempered man, and he never felt that his wife did enough in the house. One evening he came home and cursed and yelled like a bear with a sore throat.

"Please, dear, don't be so angry!" said his wife. "Tomorrow we'll swap jobs: I'll go out with the haymakers, and you can keep house."

Well, the man thought this was a good idea, and he said he would like to.

Early in the next morning the farmer's wife slung the scythe over her shoulder and went out into the field to cut hay, and the man set about tending the house.

First he thought he would churn some butter, but after a while he got thirsty and went down to the cellar to fetch some beer. While he was tapping beer into a wooden bowl, he heard the pig rummaging about in the room above. He dashed up the

cellar steps with the tap to the barrel in his hand to make sure that the pig had not upset the churn.

But when he saw that the pig had already knocked over the churn and was licking up the cream that had been spilt all over the floor, he became so angry that he forgot the barrel of beer, and chased the pig. He caught up with it just as it reached the door, and kicked it so hard it never stirred again. Then he

remembered that he still had the tap in his hand, but by the time he got to the cellar the beer barrel was empty.

He returned to the milk shed where he found enough cream to fill the churn, and kept on churning away, for he wanted to have butter for his midday meal.

After he had been churning for a while, he suddenly remembered that a cow at home in the stable still had not been fed or watered, although the sun was already high in the sky. He felt it was too far to take the cow to the field, so he thought he might as well let her graze on the roof of the farm house, where there was turf and plenty of luscious, green grass. The house was on a steep hillside, and he felt sure he would be able to get the cow up there if he laid a plank across to the roof.

But he did not dare to let go of the churn either, for he was worried that his little baby who was crawling about on the floor, might knock it over. So he hoisted the churn on his back, and went out to give the cow some water before he led it up onto the roof. Well, he grabbed a bucket to fetch water from the well, but when he bent over the side of the well, the cream poured out of the churn and ran down his neck.

137

By now dinnertime was drawing closer, and he still had no butter. So he thought he could make some porridge, and hung a pot of water over the hearth. Then the thought struck him that the cow might fall off the roof and break her legs or neck, and so he went up on the roof to tether her. He tied a loop around the cow's neck, dropped the rope down the chimney,

138

where he fastened it around his leg, for the water was already boiling in the pot and he had to start making the porridge.

While he was doing this, the cow did fall off the roof after all, and pulled the man up the chimney by his leg. There he got stuck, while the cow dangled in the air beside the wall outside, unable to get up or down.

Meanwhile, the farmer's wife had been waiting for hours for her husband to call her in for dinner, but time dragged on and

nothing happened. At last she grew tired of waiting and set off for home. As soon as she caught sight of the wretched cow hanging from the roof, she went up to it and cut the rope with her scythe. At that very moment the farmer fell down the chimney, and when his wife entered the house he was standing on his head in the porridge pot.

The Boy who wanted to marry the Daughter of the Old Woman in the Corner

Once upon a time there was an old woman who had a son, and he was so lazy and complacent that he never wanted to do anything useful. But he did like to sing and dance, and he sang and he danced all day long and half the night too. As time passed, the woman grew poorer and poorer; the boy grew bigger and needed more and more food and more and more clothes as he kept on growing, but they did not last for long, I am sure, because he was dancing and running through forests and meadows.

Eventually, the old woman decided enough was enough. So one day she told the boy that it was time for him to go out to work and do something useful, or they would both starve to death. But the lad didn't like that plan much. He said he would rather propose to the daughter of the old woman in the corner, for if he married her, he would live a happy and merry life, singing and dancing and never having to worry about work.

When his mother heard this, she thought perhaps it might not be a bad idea after all, he might as well try his luck. She cleaned up the boy as best as she could to make him look a bit respectable when he came to the old woman in the corner, and off he went.

When he left the house, the sun was shining warm and bright, but it had rained during the night, the ground was soggy and all the marshy hollows were full of water. The boy took the shortest route to the old woman in the corner, and he sang and he ran as he always did; but just as he was skipping and running, he suddenly came to a bog. There was a duckboard path across it, and when this ran out, he tried to jump from the logs to a tussock, so as not to dirty his shoes. But as his foot landed on the tussock, there was a big splash. Down he went, and did not stop until he found himself in a nasty, scary, dark hole. At first he couldn't see anything, but after he had been there a little while, he caught sight of a rat bustling and prancing around with a huge set of keys in its tail.

"Is that you, my boy?" the rat asked. "Thank you for coming to see me, I have been waiting for you for a long time. You have probably come to ask me to marry you, and you are in a hurry, I suspect, but you must be patient a little while, for I shall have a large wedding at home and I am not ready for the wedding just yet. But I shall do my best that it can be soon."

After saying that she brought out some eggshells containing all kinds of bits of food that rats like to eat and put them in front of him saying: "Sit down and have a bite to eat, you must be tired and hungry."

But the boy felt that he didn't want to eat that kind of food. If only I could get out of here and back above ground, he thought, but he didn't say a word.

"I expect you want to go back home now," said the rat. "You must be looking forward to the wedding, I suppose, and I shall hurry up as much as I can. Take this thread of linen with you, and when you are above ground, don't look back, but go straight home, and all the way home you must not say anything other than *short ahead and far behind.*" And she gave him a thread of linen in his hand.

"Thank heavens," said the boy, once he was safely back above ground. "I shall never come back here again."

And off he went with the thread in his hand, and he ran and he sang like he always did, and even though he did not give the rat's hole another thought, the phrase had stuck in his mind and he sang:

Short ahead and far behind!
Short ahead and far behind!

When he finally arrived at home in the hallway, he turned and looked behind him; there were many, many hundreds of yards of the whitest canvas cloth, so fine that not even the best weaver in the world could weave it finer.

"Mother, mother, come out and look!" he cried.

The old woman came running and asked whatever was going on. When she saw the cloth stretched out as far as the eye could see and then a bit farther, she couldn't believe her eyes, until the boy told her the whole story of how it had come to pass. Once she had heard the story and felt the cloth between her fingers, she grew so happy that she started to sing and dance, just like her son.

She brought the cloth in and cut it up into lengths and made shirts for her son and herself. The rest she took to town and sold for good money. For a while they lived very comfortably from this. But when the money ran out, the old woman had no food left in the house, and so she said to her son that now he really had to go out to work and do something useful, or they would both starve to death.

But the boy preferred to go to the old woman in the corner and ask for her daughter's hand in marriage. And his mother thought perhaps this was as good a plan as any, for now he was well dressed and didn't look too bad at all. She dressed him up and groomed him the best she could, and he took out his new shoes and polished them until they were as shiny as a mirror, and once he had done that, he set off.

It was just like the last time: When he left the house, the sun was shining and it was warm and bright, but it had rained during the night, the ground was wet and muddy and all the marshy hollows full of water. The boy took the quickest route to the old woman in the corner, and he sang and he ran as he always did. He took a different path than the previous time, but as he was skipping and running along, he suddenly came to the same wooden footpath over the bog, and just as he was trying to jump to a tussock on the other side of the next bog, so as not to dirty his shoes, there was a loud splash. Down he went, and did not stop until he found himself in a nasty, scary, dark hole. At first he couldn't see a thing, but after he had been there a little while, he caught sight of a rat carrying a set of keys in its tail and bustling and prancing around.

"Is that you, my boy?" the rat asked. "Welcome back, how kind

of you to come and see me again so soon. You are very impatient, I can tell, but you will have to bear with me a little while longer, as there are still some things to prepare for my wedding. But the next time you come, everything will be ready."

After saying that she brought out all kinds of bits to eat served in eggshells – the kind of things that rats usually eat and love, but to the boy they looked like mouldy scraps from the dinner table. He said that he was not hungry. If only I could escape from here and be above ground again, he thought, but he didn't say a word.

After a little while the rat said: "I expect you want to go back home now. I shall hurry up the wedding preparations as much as I can. But for now, take this thread of wool with you, and when you are above ground, don't look back, but go straight home, and all the way home you must not say anything other than *short ahead and far behind*." And she placed the piece of wool in his hand.

"Thank God I got out of there," said the boy to himself. "I shall never come back here again." And he ran and he sang like he always did. He did not give the rat's hole another thought, but still the phrase had stuck in his mind and he sang:

Short ahead and far behind!
Short ahead and far behind!

all the way home.

When he finally arrived at home and was on the doorstep, he turned and looked behind him; there were many, many hundreds of yards (perhaps even a mile) of the finest woollen cloth, so fine that not even the best-dressed person in town could have finer cloth for

their dresses and coats.

"Mother, mother, come out and look!" he cried.

The old woman clapped her hands together and was close to swooning with joy when she saw all the fine woollen cloth, and he had to tell her how he got it – the whole story from beginning to end.

Now they were very well off, as you can imagine. The boy got new, fine clothes, and the old woman went to town and sold the cloth a little at a time and got a great deal of money for it. Then she redecorated the cottage and became so grand in her old age that she might as well have been a lady. They lived very comfortably, but in the end the money ran out again. One day the old woman did not have any food left in the house, so she said to her son that now he really would have to go out to work and do something useful, or they would both starve to death.

But the boy thought it better to go to the old woman in the corner and ask her daughter to marry him. This time the old woman agreed with him and didn't try to dissuade him, for now he had fine new clothes, and he looked so good that she could not imagine that anyone would turn down such a handsome young man. She dressed him up and groomed him the best she could, and he brought out his new shoes and rubbed them until they were so shiny he could see his face reflected in them, and once he had done that, he set off.

This time he did not take the shortest route. He made a huge detour, as he did not want to end up underground in the rat's hole again – he had had enough of her bustling and prancing and her endless chatter about the wedding. The weather and the ground were just like the other two times. The sun shone and made the mud and marshy puddles sparkle, and the boy sang and skipped, as was his habit. But as he was skipping and running along, before he knew what had happened, he found himself on the same little wooden walkway over the bog. He was just trying to jump over a puddle to a tussock on the other side, so as not to dirty his shiny shoes, when there was a splash, and down he went, and did not stop until he found himself in the same nasty, scary hole. At first he was happy, because he seemed to be alone; but after he had been there a little while, he caught a glimpse of the ugly rat that he was trying to avoid, bustling about with her keys at the end of her tail.

"Hello, my boy," said the rat. "Welcome back. I see that you can't bear to be apart from me for long, which is very sweet. But now everything is ready for the wedding, and we must set off for the church straight away."

So what's going to happen now? thought the boy, but he didn't say anything.

Then the rat squeaked, and hundreds of small rats and mice came streaming out from all the corners, followed by six big rats pulling a large frying pan behind them. Two mice sat behind, like footmen, and two sat at the front and steered. Some of the

151

other rats and mice got into the pan, and the rat with the keys in her tail took her place in the middle.

Then she said to the boy: "The passage is a little narrow here. You will have to walk beside the carriage until the road widens out a little, my dear, then you can sit up here with me."

That'll be great! thought the boy. If only I were back above ground, I would run away from the whole riffraff, he thought, but he didn't say a word.

He followed the strange party the best he could; at times he had to crawl, and at times he had to walk bent in half, for the passage was very narrow in places. When the passage widened out, he walked in front and started looking for ways to escape from them and run away. But just as he was walking along, he heard a beautiful, clear voice behind him say: "The road is good now, come and sit in the carriage with me, my dear!"

The boy spun around on his heels and could hardly believe his eyes and ears, for behind him was the most ornate carriage he could imagine, with six white horses to pull it, and in the carriage sat a maiden as fair and lovely as the sun, surrounded by other maids as beautiful and bright as stars. It was a princess and her handmaidens that had been under a spell. But now the curse had been lifted, because he had come down to them and had not contradicted them.

"Come," said the princess. And so the boy jumped up into the carriage, and off they drove to the church.

When they left the church, the princess said: "First we will go back to my home, then we can send for your mother."

Good enough, the boy thought – he didn't say anything now either – although he was sure he would rather go home to his mother than back down into the dark, dank rat's hole. But before he knew it, they had arrived at a magnificent castle, where they entered, and were to stay. A splendid carriage with six horses was sent to fetch the old woman, and when it returned, the wedding

celebrations began. The revelries lasted for fourteen days, and who knows, perhaps they're not over yet. If we hurry, we might get there in time to drink a toast with the bridegroom and dance with the bride.

THE MYSTERIOUS BOX

Once upon a time a small boy was walking along a country road. After he had been walking for a while, he found a box. "I think there's something strange in this box," he said to himself. But no matter how he twisted and turned it, he couldn't get it open. "There must be something *really* strange in there," he thought to himself.

After he had walked a little farther, he found a tiny key and soon after he felt tired and sat down to rest. Then the thought struck him that it would be fun to see if the key fitted the lock of the box.

The boy took the tiny key, out of his pocket. First he blew on the shaft of the key, and then he blew into the keyhole. After that he put the key in the keyhole and turned it. "Click!" said the lock, and when the boy touched the lid, the box opened.

Now can you guess what was in that box?

A calf's tail.

And if the calf's tail had been any longer, then this story would have been longer, too.

THE PARSON AND THE SEXTON

Once upon a time there was a parson who was so pompous and boisterous that whenever he saw anyone come driving towards him on the road, he would shout from afar:

"Off the road! Off the road! Here comes the parson himself!"

Once while out travelling like this, he met the king.

"Off the road! Off the road!" he roared from a long way off, but the king didn't yield and kept on driving straight ahead. So, for once, the parson had to turn his horse aside.

And when the king came alongside he said:
"Tomorrow you shall come to my manor house,
and if you don't answer correctly three questions
I will put to you, you shall lose your clergyman's
frock and collar for the sake of your pride."

This was something the parson was not accustomed to. He knew how to boast and bellow, and worse than that, too. But questions and answers were not his field. So he went to the sexton, who was better known for having his wits than the parson, and told him that he had no intention of going, "for one fool can ask more than ten wise men can answer," he said. And so he got the sexton to go in his place.

Well, the sexton went; and he came to the royal manor dressed in the parson's gown and collar. The king met him out on the porch, wearing both crown and sceptre, and looking so grand he fairly shone.

"So, here you are then?" said the king.

Yes, he was … That was sure enough.

"Now, tell me first," said the king, "how far is it from east to west?"

"That's a day's journey," said the sexton.

"How's that?" asked the king.

"Well, the sun rises in the east and sets in the west, and does it nicely in a day," said the sexton.

"All right," said the king. "But tell me this," he said, "how much do you think I'm worth as I appear before you?"

"Well, Christ was valued at thirty pieces of silver, so I'd better not set you any higher than …twenty-nine," said the sexton.

"Well, well!" said the king. "Since you're such a wise man, tell me what I'm thinking now!"

"Oh, I suppose you're thinking that it is the parson who's standing here before you. But I'm sorry to say you're wrong, for I'm the sexton!"

"Really!" said the king. "Then I want you to go home and become parson and let him be sexton!" And so it was!

THE HOUSE
MOUSE AND THE
COUNTRY MOUSE

Once upon a time there were a house mouse and a country mouse. They met at the edge of the forest. The country mouse sat in a hazel bush gathering nuts.

"God bless your work!" said the house mouse. "I wasn't aware that I had relatives way out in the country?"

"Indeed you do!" replied the country mouse.

"I see you're gathering nuts and taking them home," said the house mouse.

"I have to, otherwise we won't have anything to live on during the winter," said the country mouse.

"The husks are big, and the shells are bursting this year, so they'll help to fill hungry stomachs," said the house mouse.

"That's very true," said the country mouse, and she went on to claim that she lived comfortably and was well off. The house mouse argued that she was better off, but the country mouse stood her ground, and said that no place was as good as the forest and the mountains, and that she was the one who fared the best. The house mouse insisted *she* was better off, and the two of them just could not agree as to which one had the better

life. At last they decided to visit one another at Christmas so that they could see for themselves which one was better off.

The house mouse was the first mouse to pay the other a Christmas visit. She journeyed through forests and deep valleys, and even though the country mouse had moved down the

171

mountain for the winter, the way was both long and hard. The
house mouse had an uphill struggle, and as the snow was deep

172

and loose, she grew both tired and hungry before she reached
the home of the country mouse.

I'm looking forward to a good meal now, she thought when she arrived. The country mouse had gathered together a fair amount of food. There were nut kernels, and many kinds of roots, as well as all sorts of goodies that grow in fields and forests. She had it all stored in a hole way below ground to prevent it from freezing, and not far away there was a sheltered

spring where she could drink as much water as she wanted.

Although there was enough of what there was, and they both had their fill, the house mouse thought it no more than the bare necessities of life.

"One may survive on this food," she said. "But it's not particularly good. I'd like you to come to see me, and taste my food."

Well, the country mouse said she would do this, and it wasn't long before she paid her visit. The house mouse had gathered together all the food the mistress of the house had spilled during Christmas preparations. There were pieces of cheese, butter and tallow, and crumbs of buttered bannock and oatcakes spread with cream. In the pan set underneath the beer tap she had plenty of drink, and the whole of her parlour was filled with all kinds of good food.

The two mice had a feast, and the country mouse had a seemingly endless appetite. Never before had she tasted such food. Then she became thirsty, for the food was both rich and

fat, she said, and now she needed a drink.

"The beer isn't far away. This is where we drink," said the house mouse, and she leapt up onto the edge of the pan. But

as soon as her thirst was quenched, she stopped drinking, for she knew the Christmas beer and knew it was strong.

But the country mouse had never drunk anything other than water and she thought it was a marvellous drink, and took one sip after the other. She wasn't used to strong drink, so she was tipsy before she even came down off the pan. Then the beer went straight to her head, and then to her feet, and she started running and jumping from one beer barrel to the next, and dancing and frolicking on the shelves among the cups and mugs, and squeaking and whistling as though she were both drunk and mad – and drunk she was, too.

"You mustn't act as though you've just come out of the
mountain today," said the house mouse. "Don't make such a

fuss and don't make so much noise," she said, "for we've got quite a strict bailiff here."

The country mouse said she had no respect for either bailiff or tramp.

But the cat, who was sitting on the cellar door listening, heard both the chattering and the commotion. And when the mistress of the house went down to tap beer into the jug, and

lifted up the door, the cat darted into the cellar and pounced on the country mouse. And now she danced to another tune.

The house mouse popped into her hole, from where she sat safely watching the country mouse, who soon sobered up when she felt the cat's claws.

"Oh, my dear bailiff! My dear bailiff! Have mercy on me and spare my life, and I'll tell you a story," she said.

"Out with it!" said the cat.

"Once upon a time there were two little mice," squeaked the country mouse, slowly and so pitiably, for she wanted to drag it out as long as she could.

"Then they weren't alone!" said the cat, curtly and crossly.

"Then we had a roast we were going to roast for ourselves."

"Then you didn't go hungry!" said the cat.

"Then we put it out on the roof to cool off," said the country mouse.

"Then you didn't burn yourselves," said the cat.

"Then the fox and the crow came and took it and ate it," said the country mouse.

"Then I'm going to eat you!" said the cat.

But at that very moment the mistress of the house slammed the cellar door, and this startled the cat so much that he let go of the mouse. Whoosh! The country mouse darted into the hole of the house mouse. From there she went right out into the snow, and in no time at all she was heading for home.

"You call this being well off, and say that you live best?" the country mouse said to the house mouse. "I'd rather be blessed with less then, instead of such a big manor and such a hawk for a bailiff. Why, I nearly lost my life!"

THE MILL
THAT GRINDS AT
THE BOTTOM OF
THE SEA

Once upon a time, a very long time ago, there were two brothers – one was rich and the other was poor. When Christmas Eve came, the poor brother did not have a crumb of food in his house, neither meat nor fish nor bread, and he went to his brother and asked for a little food for Christmas, for mercy's sake. I suppose this was not the first time his brother had to help him, but he was miserly by nature and was not happy to see him this time either.

"If you do what I ask, I'll give you a whole side of ham," he said. The poor brother agreed on the spot and thanked him too.

"Here it is. And now go straight to hell!" said the rich brother and threw the ham at him.

"Well, I suppose I'd better keep my promise," the other brother said, he took the ham and set off.

He walked and he walked, all day long, and at dusk he came to a place that was lit up brightly. This must be it, thought the man with the ham. In the woodshed an old man with a long white beard was cutting wood for Christmas.

"Good evening!" said the man with the ham.

"Good evening to you too! Where are you heading so late at night?" asked the old man.

"Oh, I'm on my way to hell, if I'm on the right road," answered the poor man.

"Oh yes, you're on the right road. It's here," said the other. "When you get inside, they will all want to buy your ham, as a juicy piece of meat is rare in hell. But you must not sell it, unless you get the mill standing behind the door for it. When you come out again, I will teach you how to stop the mill. It can be used for all sorts of different things, that mill".

The man with the ham thanked the old man for his good advice and knocked on the Devil's door.

When he entered, things went as the old man had predicted. All the devils, large and small, were all over him like ants or flies or worms, each making a higher offer than the last for the ham. "Well, you see, my wife and I were supposed to have it for Christmas dinner, but since you are so keen, I suppose I could give it to you," said the man. "But I'll only sell it for the hand

mill behind the door over there."

The Devil didn't want to part with the mill and bargained and haggled, but the man held his own, and so the Devil had to give it to him. When the man came out in the courtyard, he asked the old woodcutter how to stop the mill, and once he had learned that, he thanked him and set off for home as fast as he could. But he didn't make it home before the clock struck midnight on Christmas Eve.

"Where on earth have you been?" his wife asked him. "I've been sitting here for hours on end, worrying and waiting, without having so much as two twigs of firewood to put under the pot of Christmas porridge."

"I couldn't come earlier, I had all sorts of things to do and a long trip too. But wait till you see what I've got!" said the man and put the mill on the table. First he asked it to grind light, then a tablecloth, and then food and ale and all sorts of good things that people eat on Christmas Eve, and the mill ground everything he asked for.

The old woman crossed herself and crossed herself again and wanted to know where the man had got the mill from, but he wouldn't tell her. "It doesn't matter where I got it from; you can see the mill is good, and the water that turns it will never freeze," said the man. And then he ground out food and drink and all the good things that people eat for Christmas, and on the third day he invited his friends to a banquet.

190

When the rich brother saw all the good things in the banqueting hall, he grew quite wild with rage, for he could not bear for his brother to have anything.

"On Christmas Eve, he was in such need that he came to me and begged for a little food for mercy's sake, and now he is giving a feast as if he were both a count and a King all at once," he said. "But where the hell did you get all your riches from?" he asked.

"From behind the door," said the man who owned the mill, for he didn't care to give account to him, oh no.

But as the evening wore on and his head began to be heavy from too much drink, he could not help himself and brought out the mill. "This is what brought me all my riches!" he said, and then he made the mill grind one thing after another.

When his brother saw this, he wanted to have the mill more than anything in this life or the next, and eventually he would have it too, although it would cost him three hundred specie dollars and the one was to keep it until the haymaking season. For by then I have had it long enough to have milled all I need for many years to come, he thought. During that time the mill did not grow rusty, as you may imagine, and when haymaking was due, the brother got it, but the other had taken care not to teach him how to stop it.

It was evening when the rich brother finally got the mill home, and in the morning he told his wife to go out and spread the hay behind the mowers; he would make lunch himself today, he said.

When it was almost lunchtime, he placed the mill on the table.

"Grind herring and gruel, and make it snappy!" said the man. And the mill started to grind herring and gruel, first filling all the plates and troughs to the brim, and then spilling out over the kitchen floor. The man fiddled and meddled and tried to make the mill stop, but no matter how he turned it and tuned it, the mill kept on grinding, and soon there was so much gruel that the man was about to drown. Then he pulled open the door to the sitting room, although it was not easy for him to reach the latch down in the ocean of gruel. When he finally opened the door, he did not stay in the sitting room very long, I would imagine. He rushed out of the house, with the herring and gruel behind him in a giant wave that crashed over the farm and the fields.

Now his wife, who was working hard spreading the hay, thought it was taking an awfully long time for lunch to be ready. "If my husband doesn't call us home soon, we'll have to go anyway. He doesn't know much about cooking gruel, and I'll probably have to help him," said the farmer's wife to the mowers.

And so they began to wander homewards. But when they had come a little way up the hill, they were met by herring and gruel and bread all tumbling down together, and with the farmer himself before the flood.

"I wish each of you had a hundred bellies! But watch out so you don't drown in the lunch gruel," he cried as he ran past

them as if the devil himself was at his heels, towards where his brother lived. He begged him, for mercy's sake, to take the mill back and to take it back now.

"If it grinds for another hour, the entire village will be drowned in herring and gruel," he said. But his brother refused to take it back until the other paid him another three hundred specie dollars, which he had to do.

Now the poor brother had both money and mill, and before long he had built himself a farm even grander than the one his brother lived in. He used the mill to grind so much gold for himself that he covered the entire farmhouse in sheets of gold, and since his farm lay by the sea shore, it shone and glittered for a long way over the fjord. Everyone who sailed past simply had to stop and visit the rich man in the gold house, and everybody wanted to see the magic mill, for word about it had spread far and wide, and there was nobody that had not heard about it.

After a very long time, a skipper turned up who wanted to see the mill. He asked if it could make salt. "Why, of course it can make salt!" said the man who owned it. And when the skipper heard that, he wanted the mill more than anything else, by whatever means and at whatever price. For if he owned the mill, he thought, he wouldn't have to sail far away across the seas and waves for cargos of salt. To begin with the man didn't want to part with it, but the skipper begged and pleaded, and in the end he sold it and got many, many thousands of specie dollars for it.

As soon as the skipper had got the mill on his back, he set off as quickly as he could, for he feared that the man might change his mind. He had no time to ask how to stop it; he hurried to his ship as fast as he could, and only when he was a good way out to sea, did he set up the mill.

"Grind salt, and make it snappy!" said the skipper. And sure enough, the mill started to grind salt so quickly that it flew out of the mill. When the skipper's ship was full, he wanted to stop the mill, but no matter what he tried and how he fiddled with it, the mill continued to grind away, and the mountain of salt grew higher and higher until the ship sank to the bottom of the sea.

And this very day the mill is still down there at the bottom of the sea grinding away, and that is why the sea is salty.

"Good day,
Fellow!"
"Axe Handle"

Once upon a time there was a ferryman who was so deaf
that he could neither hear nor make out what anyone
said to him.

197

He had a wife, and two sons and a daughter, but they didn't bother themselves about the man. They lived a jolly life and they lived well, as long as they had something to live on. And afterwards they got credit from the innkeeper, and gave parties and feasts every day.

When there was no one willing to give them any more credit, the district sheriff was coming to seize their goods to pay for

what they had borrowed and wasted. The old woman and the children went to her relatives, leaving the deaf man behind on his own to receive the sheriff and his assistant.

The man poked and pottered about the place, and wondered what the sheriff wanted to ask about, and what he should say when he came.

"I can start whittling away at something," he said to himself. "Then he'll ask me about it. I'll start whittling an axe handle. Then he'll ask me what it's going to be, and I'll say: 'Axe handle!' Then he'll ask me how long it's going to be, and I'll say: 'Up to this knot!' Then he'll ask me where the ferry is, and I'll say: 'I'm going to tar her. She's lying down on the shore, cracked at both ends!'

Then he'll ask: 'Where's that old grey mare of yours?' So I'll say: 'She's out in the stall, big with foal!' Then he'll ask: 'Where are your cattle and your cowshed?' And I'll say: 'That's not far from here. Once you get up the hill, you'll be there in no time!'

To his way of thinking, this plan was well and carefully thought out.

Shortly afterwards the sheriff arrived. He was safe enough, but his assistant had taken another route by way of the inn, and was still sitting there drinking.

"Good day, man!" said the sheriff.

"Axe handle!" said the ferryman.

"Really?" said the sheriff, and then he asked: "How far is it to the inn?"

"Up to this knot!" said the man and pointed some way up the axe handle.

The sheriff shook his head and stared severely at him.

"Where's your wife, man?" he said.

"I'm going to tar her," said the ferryman. "She's lying down on the shore, cracked at both ends!"

"Where's your daughter?"

"Oh, she's out in the stall, big with foal!" said the man, who thought he was answering both wisely and well for himself.

"Oh, go to hell, fool that you are!" said the sheriff.

"Well, that's not far from here. Once you get up the hill, you'll be there in no time!" said the man.

THE DOLL
IN THE GRASS

Once upon a time there was a king who had twelve sons.
When they were grown up, he told them to go out into the
world and find themselves wives, but these wives must each be

able to spin and weave and sew a shirt in one day, or else he wouldn't have them for daughters-in-law. To each he gave a horse and a new suit of armour, and they went out into the world to look for their brides.

But when they had gone part of the way, they said they didn't

want Cinderlad, their youngest brother, to travel with them, for he wasn't fit for anything.

So Cinderlad had to stay behind, and he didn't know what to do or whither to turn. He grew so downcast that he got off his horse, and sat down in the tall grass to weep. But when he had sat there a little while, one of the tufts of grass began to move, and out of it came a little white thing. And when it came nearer, Cinderlad saw that it was a charming little girl, only she was such a tiny thing.

The girl walked across to him, and asked if he would come down and see the Doll in the Grass.

Yes, he'd be very happy to do so!

Now, when he got down, the Doll in the Grass was sitting on a chair. She was so lovely and so pretty, and she asked Cinderlad where he was going, and what was his business.

He told her how they were twelve brothers, and how the king had given them horses and armour, and told them that each of them must go out into the world and find himself a wife who could spin and weave and sew a shirt in one day. "But if you'll only say right now that you'll be my wife, I'll not go a step further," said Cinderlad to the Doll in the Grass.

208

Yes, she was more than willing, and so she made haste and span, and wove, and sewed the shirt, but it was so very, very tiny. It wasn't longer more than so – – – long.

So Cinderlad set off home with this shirt, but when he brought it out, he was ashamed, for it was so small. Still the king said he should have her, and so Cinderlad set off, glad and happy to fetch his little sweetheart.

And when he got to the Doll in the Grass, he wanted to take her up before him on his horse; but she wouldn't have that, for she said she would sit and drive along in a silver spoon, and that she had two small white horses to draw her.

So off they set, he on his horse and she in her silver spoon, and
the two horses that drew her, were two tiny white mice. But

Cinderlad always kept to the other side of the road, for she was
so little that he was afraid he might ride over her.

When they had gone a part of the way, they came to a great stretch of water. There Cinderlad's horse got frightened, and shied across the road and upset the spoon, and the Doll in the Grass tumbled into the water.

Cinderlad was so sorrowful, because he didn't know how to get her out again. But shortly afterwards a merman appeared with

her, and now she was as full grown as other men and women, and far lovelier than she had been before. So he took her up before him on his horse, and rode home.

When Cinderlad got home, all his brothers had returned, each with his sweetheart, but these were all so ugly, and foul, and so wicked that they had done nothing but fight with one another on the way home, and on their heads they had a kind of hat that was daubed over with tar and soot, and so the rain had run down off the hats onto their faces, till they grew far uglier and nastier than they had been before.

When his brothers saw Cinderlad and his sweetheart, they were all as jealous as jealous could be of her. But the king was so

overjoyed with them both, that he drove all the others away, and
so Cinderlad held his wedding feast with the Doll in the Grass,
and they both lived happily ever after. And if they're not dead,
then they're still alive.

LITTLE FRIKK
AND HIS FIDDLE

Once upon a time there was a poor farmer who had only one son, and this boy was so skinny and weak and in such poor health that he was not able to work. His name was Frikk, and he was so small that they called him Little Frikk.

At home there was little to eat and little to do, so his father went to all the neighbouring farms to see if he could hire him out as a shepherd or errand boy. But nobody wanted his boy, until he came to the sheriff's house. He decided to take Little Frikk, as he had recently chased off his errand boy, and nobody else was willing to work for him as he had a reputation of being a rogue. It was better than nothing, the farmer thought to himself. At least the boy would be fed there, because he was to serve food at the sheriff's, with no question of wages or clothes. After the boy had been there for three years, he wanted to leave, and then the sheriff gave him his wages all at once. He was paid one shilling for each year he had worked – it couldn't be less, said the sheriff. So he got a total of three shillings.

Little Frikk thought this was an awful lot of money, for he had never owned so much, but he asked if he wasn't to have more.

"You've already had more than you should have," said the sheriff.

"Shouldn't I get something to buy clothes with?" asked Little Frikk. "I have worn out the clothes I had when I arrived here, and I haven't been given anything in return," he said. Now his clothes were so ragged they hung off him in tatters and flapped in the wind, he said.

"You have received what we agreed on and three shillings ex- tra, and now I don't want to have any more to do with you," said the sheriff. But he was allowed to go into the kitchen for a little food for his haversack, and then he set off on the road to town to go and buy some clothes. He was in high spirits, for he had ne- ver seen a shilling before, and every now and again, he looked if he still had all three.

When he had walked a long way and then a bit more, he came to a narrow valley with high mountains on all sides, and he could see no way to pass. He wondered what could be on the other side of these mountains, and how to cross them. But one thing was certain, he would have to go uphill, and off he set. He was not good for much and had to stop and rest from time to time, and then he counted how much money he had. When he finally got to the top, there was nothing there apart from a moss-covered mountain plateau. There he sat down and was about to make sure he still had all his shillings, and before he knew what had happened, a pauper came to him. The pauper was so big and so tall that the boy started to scream when he saw just how big and tall he was.

"Don't be scared, lad," said the pauper, "I won't harm you. All I want is a shilling, for mercy's sake!"

"Gracious," said the boy, "I only have three shillings, and I'm on my way to town to buy clothes with them," he said.

"I'm worse off than you," said the pauper. "I don't have any shillings, and my clothes are even more ragged than yours."

"Well, I suppose you'd better have it, then," said the boy.

After he had been walking for a while, he grew tired and sat down to rest again. When he looked up, there was another pauper in front of him, but this one was even bigger and even uglier than the first beggar, and when the boy saw just how ugly and tall he was, he started to scream.

"Don't be scared of me. I won't harm you. All I want is a shilling, for mercy's sake!" said the pauper.

"Goodness gracious," said the boy, "I only have two shillings, and I'm on my way to town to buy clothes with them. If I had only met you earlier …"

"I'm worse off than you," said the beggar. "I don't have any shillings, and I have a bigger body and fewer clothes than you."

"Well, I suppose you'd better have it then," said the boy.

Then he walked for a little while again until he was tired, and then he sat down to rest. As soon as he had sat down again, a third pauper came to him. He was so big and so ugly and so tall that the boy looked up and up until he was looking straight up into the sky, and when he saw just how ugly and ragged he was, he started to scream.

"Don't be scared of me, lad," said the man. "I won't harm you. I am just a poor beggar who wants a shilling, for mercy's sake!"

"Goodness gracious," said Little Frikk. "I only have one shilling left, and I'm on my way to town to buy clothes with it. If I had only met you earlier …"

"Yes, but I don't have any shillings, and I have a bigger body and fewer clothes, so I'm worse off than you," said the beggar.

So he'd better have the shilling, then, said Little Frikk, it can't be helped, now each had their shilling and he had none.

"Well, since you have such a good heart that you gave away everything you owned," said the pauper, "I shall grant you one wish for every shilling." The same pauper had received all three coins, but he had changed his appearance each time for the boy not to recognize him.

"I've always wanted so hard to hear the sound of the fiddle and watch people become so merry and happy that they dance," said the boy. "So, if I can have whatever I wish for, I wish for a fiddle that makes everyone dance to it," he said.

His wish would be granted, but it was a pretty poor wish, said the pauper. "You should wish for something better for the other shillings."

"I've always wanted so hard to hunt and shoot," said Little Frikk. "So, if I can have whatever I wish for, I wish for a rifle that hits everything I aim at, no matter how far away."

His wish would be granted, but it was a pretty poor wish, said the pauper. "You should wish for something better for the last shilling."

"I've always wanted so badly to be among people who were

kind and good-hearted," said Little Frikk. "So, if I can have whatever I wish for, I wish that nobody can refuse the first thing that I ask for."

"Now that wish was better," said the pauper, and then he rushed off between the hills and was gone, and the boy lay down to sleep, and the next day he came down from the mountain with his fiddle and rifle.

First he went to the general store and asked for clothes, and at one farm he asked for a horse, and at another he asked for a sleigh, and somewhere he asked for a coat made of reindeer skin, and nobody could say no to him, not even the greatest miser of them all – they had to give him what he asked for. Finally, he travelled through the parish like a fine gentleman with his horse and sleigh.

After travelling for a while, he met the sheriff he had worked for.

"Good day, master," said Little Frikk with his fiddle, stopping to greet him.

"Good day," said the sheriff. "Have *I* been your master?" he asked.

"Yes, don't you remember that I served you for three years for three shillings?" said Little Frikk.

"Good heavens, you have come up in the world quickly, then," said the sheriff. "How have you managed to become such a grand gentleman?"

"Well, you know how it is," said the little lad.

"Are you such a merry man of leisure that you play the fiddle too?" said the sheriff.

"Yes, I have always wanted to make people dance," said the boy. "But the finest thing I have is this rifle," he said. "It falls, most everything I point it at, no matter how far away it is. Do you see that magpie sitting in the spruce tree over there?" said Little Frikk. "How much do you bet that I hit it from where we are standing?" he asked.

In that case the sheriff would gladly bet his horse and his farm and one hundred dollars that he would not make it, but he would bet all the money he had on him there and then, and he would even go and get the bird when it fell, for he was sure it was impossible to shoot something at that distance, whatever kind of gun you had. But the moment the gun banged, the magpie fell down into a large thicket of brambles, and the sheriff set off into the brambles for it. He picked up the bird to bring it back to the boy, but just then Little Frikk started to play his fiddle, and the sheriff had to dance right there in the middle of the thicket, the thorns scratching him. The boy played, and the sheriff danced and wept and begged for mercy until the rags were torn off him and he was scarcely wearing a stitch.

"You see? Now *you* are as ragged as *I* was when I left your service," said the boy, "and that's good enough for me." But first the sheriff had to give him what he had bet that Little Frikk couldn't hit the magpie.

When the boy arrived in town, he put up at a guesthouse. He played his fiddle, and the people who came there danced, and he lived a happy and good life. He never had any cares, because nobody could say no to the first thing he asked for.

But just as everyone was having a lovely time, the guards came to arrest Little Frikk and take him to the town hall. The sheriff had complained about him, saying Little Frikk had attacked him and robbed him and nearly killed him, and now he was to be hanged, and there was no question of mercy. But Little Frikk had the solution to any problem – his fiddle. He started to play, and the guards had to dance, and keep on until they lay spent and panting on the floor. Then they sent soldiers to get him, but they fared no better than the guards. When Little Frikk took out his fiddle, they had to dance as long as he had the energy to play; but they were done for long before that.

Finally they sneaked up on him one night while he was sleeping and when they had caught him, he was sentenced to be hanged immediately and was carried off to the gallows at once. A crowd quickly gathered to watch the spectacle, and the sheriff was there too, and he was beyond himself with joy that he would be given justice for his money and his skin and watch the boy hang.

224

But things did not happen fast, for Little Frikk was frail and bad at walking, and he made himself look even frailer. He also carried his fiddle and his rifle, as nobody managed to take them from him. When he got to the gallows and was to climb up the ladder, he stopped to rest on each rung. On the top of the ladder he sat down and asked if they could deny him a final wish, if they wouldn't allow him one last thing. He wanted to play a playful tune on his fiddle before they hanged him.

"Why of course, it would be a shame and a sin to refuse him that," they said, for they could not say no to whatever he asked for. But the sheriff begged for mercy's sake not to let him so much as pluck a single string, or they would all be done for. Would the boy be allowed to play, they would have to tie *him* to the birch tree standing there. Little Frikk did not hesitate to play his fiddle, and everyone there started to dance, both the two-legged and the four-legged, both rector and priest, recorder and bailiff, and sheriff and masters and dogs and swines. They danced and laughed and shouted. Some danced until they collapsed as if they were dead, and some danced until they fell down in a faint. It went badly for them all, but worst for the sheriff, for he was tied to the birch tree, dancing off large parts of his back against the tree trunk. Nobody tried to stop Little Frikk, and he was allowed to go with his rifle and his fiddle as he pleased, and he lived happily ever after, because nobody could say no to the first thing he asked for.

THE FOX AS SHEPHERD

Once upon a time there was a woman who was on her way
to hire a shepherd when she met a bear.

"Where are you off to?" said the bear.

"Oh, I'm off to hire myself a shepherd," replied the woman.

"Wouldn't you like me to be your shepherd?" asked the bear.

"Yes, if only you know how to call the animals," said the

woman. "Grrrr," growled the bear.

"No, you're of no use!" said the woman when she heard that, and went away.

After she had walked along for some time, she met a wolf.

"Where are you off to?" said the wolf.

"I'm going to hire myself a shepherd," said the woman.

"Would you like me to be your shepherd?" asked the wolf.

"Yes, if you know how to call the animals," said the woman.

"Ouh, ouh, ouh!" said the wolf.

"Oh, no! I don't want you," she said.

When she had gone a little further, she met a fox.

"Where are you off to?" asked the fox.

"Oh, I'm looking for a shepherd to hire," replied the woman.

"Will you hire me as your shepherd?" asked the fox.

"Yes, if only you know how to call the animals," the woman said.

"Dilly, dally, holly, dolly," cried the fox in a clear and ringing voice.

"Yes, you're just the right fellow I need for a shepherd," said the woman, and she hired the fox.

The first day the fox herded the livestock, he gobbled up all the woman's goats. The next day he ate up all her sheep, and on the third day he gobbled up all her cows. When he came home that evening, the woman asked what he had done with all her animals.

"Their skulls are in the river and their bones are in the woods," said the fox.

The woman was busy churning butter, but she thought she should go outside to see what had happened to all her animals, and while she was gone, the fox popped down in the churn and ate up the cream.

When the woman returned home and saw what the fox had done, she became so angry that she took the tiny drop of cream left, and threw it at the fox, so he got a drop on the tip of his tail.

And that is why the fox has a white tip on his tail.

The Princess on the Glass Mountain

Once upon a time there was a man who had an outlying field on the mountainside somewhere, and in this field was a barn to keep his hay in. But there hadn't been much in the barn for the last few years, I am sure, because each Midsummer Night, when the grass was at its lushest and richest, the meadow was chewed bare as if a whole herd of animals had grazed there overnight. It happened once, and it happened twice. But then the man became tired of this and said to his sons – he had three, and the third one was called Cinderlad, as if you didn't already know – that one of them would have to sleep in the hay loft in the mountain field on Midsummer Night, so that the grass would not be eaten right down to the stubble like the last two years. And whoever got the job would have to be very vigilant, the man said.

Well, of course, the eldest son wanted to tend the field. He would look after the grass, he said, so that neither man nor beast nor even the devil himself would take any of it. When evening came, he went over to the barn and went to sleep. But later in the night there was a loud rumbling and an earthquake shaking the walls and the roof of the barn. The boy got up and was on the run quicker than ever. He didn't even dare to look around, and the hay was eaten up that night, like the last two years.

Next Midsummer Night the man said again that it was not right that year after year they lost the crop of hay from the outlying field. One of his sons would have to keep watch – and this time properly. Now the second son wanted a chance to prove himself that evening. He went across to the hay barn and lay down to sleep, as his brother had done the year before. But later in the night there was a loud rumbling, and the earth shook even worse than last Midsummer Night. And when the poor lad heard it, he was terrified and set off running as if his life depended on it.

The following year it was the Cinderlad's turn, but while he was getting ready to leave, his two brothers laughed at him and made fun of him.

"Oh yes, you're certainly the right man to guard the hay – you don't know anything but sitting among the ashes and toast yourself!" they mocked.

But the Cinderlad did not worry about their words, and when evening drew on, he wandered over to the field. When he got there, he went into the hay barn and lay down to sleep. But after a while, there was a huge roar and a thundering sound.

Well, if it doesn't get any worse, I can bear it, thought Cinderlad. After a little while there was another crash, and the earth shook so hard the hay flew around the boy.

Well, if it doesn't get any worse, I can bear it, thought Cinderlad. Loudest of all was the third roar, accompanied by such a powerful earthquake that the boy expected the walls and roof of the barn to fall down upon him. But when it was all over, it was dead silent.

"I expect it will be back again soon," thought Cinderlad. But no, it didn't come back. It was quiet and it stayed quiet, and when he had lain there a little while, he thought he heard the sound of a horse chewing right outside the barn door. He stole over to the crack in the door to see what it was. And sure enough, a horse was standing there nibbling away, but Cinderlad had never seen such an enormous, strong, fine horse before. It was carrying a saddle and bridle, and a full suit of armour for a knight, and everything was made of copper and so shiny that it gleamed.

Ho ho, so it's *you* who have been eating up all our hay, is it? thought the boy. But I can't let you do that.

He quickly got his fire flint out and waved it over the horse, so that the horse lost his power to move from the spot. Now it was so tame that the boy could do with it as he pleased. He mounted the horse and rode it to a secret place nobody knew about, and there he kept it.

When he returned back home, his brothers laughed and asked how he had fared.

"I bet you didn't stay asleep in the hay barn for long, if you even went out as far as the field," they said.

"I lay in the hay barn until the sun came streaming in, I did, but I neither heard nor saw anything," said the boy. "I wonder what frightened you two so hard!"

"Well, let's go and see how well you managed to look after the field," the brothers replied. But when they got there, they found the grass still standing as the evening before.

Next Midsummer Night, it was the same story: Neither of the two elder brothers dared to go over to the outlaying field to look after the grass, but the Cinderlad dared. And things happened exactly as they had happened last Midsummer Night: First there was a loud rumbling and then an earthquake, followed by another, and a third. But this time, the three earthquakes were much, much stronger. Then all of a sudden it was deadly silent, and the boy heard something chewing outside the barn door. He stole over to the crack in the door as slowly as he could. And there it was – another horse stood there munching and chomping away, and it was even larger and stronger than the first horse. It had a saddle on its back, and a bridle and a full set of armour for a knight, all made of silver and as magnificent as anyone had ever seen.

Ho ho, so it's *you* who are eating up all our hay tonight, is it? thought the boy. But I can't let you do that.

He took his flint and waved it over the horse's mane, and then the horse stood there as tame as a lamb. The boy rode it to where he kept the first horse, and then he went back home.

"I bet the hay field is a pretty sight this morning, eh?" said the brothers.

"But of course!" said Cinderlad.

They had to go and look for themselves, and sure enough, the grass was as thick and as tall as before, but that didn't make them any kinder to Cinderlad.

When the third Midsummer Night came around, neither of the two elder brothers dared to sleep in the barn and watch the grass; they had had such a fright the night they were there, that they never forgot it. But Cinderlad dared. And it was the same as the last two Midsummer Nights: There were three earthquakes, each stronger than the last. The final earthquake was so violent that the boy was thrown back and forth from one wall of the barn to the other. But then, all of a sudden, everything went deadly silent. When he had lain there for a little while, he heard the sound of something chewing outside the barn door. He stole over to the crack in the door again and saw a horse standing right outside that was much, much larger and much, much stronger than both of the other two horses he had caught, with a bridle and saddle and a full set of armour made of pure, red gold.

Ho ho, so it's *you* who is eating up all our hay this time, is it? thought the boy. But I can't let you do that.

He took out his flint and waved it over the horse's mane, and then the horse stood there as if it were nailed to the ground, and the boy could do with it as he pleased. He rode it to where he kept the other two horses, and then went back home. There, his two brothers made fun of him, just like the other times. He must have spent a pleasant night in the mountain field, they said, because he looked still asleep. But Cinderlad ignored them. He told them to go and see for themselves. This time too they found the grass as lush and deep as the day before.

Now, the king of the country where Cinderlad's father lived, had a daughter, and he would only give her to the person who could ride up the mountain hill – for there was a towering glass as smooth as ice not far from the manor house. The princess would sit at the very top of the mountain, with three golden apples in her lap, and whoever could ride up and take the three golden apples, would have her hand in marriage and half the kingdom. The king put out word of this outside every church in the entire country and in many other kingdoms too. Now, the princess was so beautiful that everyone who saw her, fell in love with her – whether they wanted to or not – and so, as you may imagine, all the princes and knights wanted to win her and half the kingdom to boot. They came riding from all four corners of the earth, dressed in all kinds of magnificent costumes and on proud, prancing horses that were a pleasure to ride. And of course, each of them was sure that *he* would be the one to win the princess's hand.

When the day came that the king had chosen, such a crowd of knights and princes had gathered at the foot of the glass hill that it was swarming with them. And then everything that could walk, on two legs or four, wanted to go there to see who would win the king's daughter. Cinderlad's two brothers also wanted to watch the spectacle, but they certainly didn't want to have *him* with them. If they were seen with such an oaf, so dirty from poking around in the ashes all day, people would laugh at them, they said.

"Well, I am as happy going alone by myself, I am," said Cinderlad.

When the two brothers arrived at the glass mountain, all the princes and knights were riding until their horses were frothing. But, believe me, it didn't do them much good, for as soon as the horses put a hoof on the mountain, they slipped. Not one of them made it as far as a yard up the mountain. No wonder, for the mountain was as smooth as a pane of glass and as steep as a wall. But the princess and half the kingdom they all wanted, and so they kept on riding and slipping, riding and slipping, without fail. In the end, all the horses were so exhausted they could not move, and so sweat they were dripping, and the riders had to give up. The king was already considering to proclaim the riding to begin again next day, in the hope that it might improve. But at that very moment, a knight came along on the finest horse anyone had ever seen. He had copper armour and a copper bridle, so shiny it gleamed. The others shouted out to him that he might as well save himself the bother of

242

trying to ride up the glass mountain, for it was impossible. But he chose not to hear them. He galloped straight towards the glass mountain and rode up as if it was the easiest thing in the world, a good way up, perhaps as much as a third of the way up, then he turned his horse around and rode down again. The king's daughter thought he was the handsomest knight she had ever seen, and as he rode up towards her, she sat there and thought to herself: I hope he makes it! And when she saw that he was turning his horse back, she threw one of the golden apples after him, and it rolled into his shoe. But as soon as he was down from the glass hill, he rode away, so quickly that nobody knew what had become of him.

That evening all the princes and knights were to show up before the King; the one who had reached that far up the glass mountain, was to present the golden apple that the princess had thrown down. But none of them had anything to show. One after another paraded in front of the King, but none of them had the apple.

Later that evening Cinderlad's brothers went home too and told forth about the riding up the glass mountain, how at first nobody could ride so much as a step up the hill.

"But then a knight came along who had a copper armour and a copper bridle so bright that they gleamed from way off," they said.

"Now, *he* knew how to ride! He rode more than one third of the glass mountain, and he probably could have ridden all the way up, if he had wanted to. But he turned his horse around, for he must have found it enough for now."

243

"Gosh, I too would have liked to see *him*," said Cinderlad, as he sat in the hearth and poked around in the ashes, like he always did.

"Huh, *you!*" said the brothers. "As if you could go out among such fine folk, you ugly beast. You stay where you are!"

The next day the brothers went off to watch the riding again, and this time too, Cinderlad asked them to let him go with them. But no, there was no way they would take him, because he was too ugly and dirty, they said.

"Well, then, I'm as happy going alone by myself, I am," said Cinderlad.

When the brothers arrived at the glass mountain, all the princes and knights started to ride again, and no doubt they had reshod their horses. But it didn't help. They rode and they slipped, like the day before, and no one made it as far as a yard up the mountain. When they had pounded their horses so hard they could no more, they all had to give up. The king considered to proclaim the riding contest to continue for the last time tomorrow, hoping it might go better then. But then he thought again: Perhaps he should wait a little in case the knight in the copper armour would show up today too. They couldn't see him anywhere, but just then a knight came along on a horse much, much finer than the one ridden by the knight in the copper armour, this one with a silver armour and a silver saddle and a silver bridle, glittering and gleaming brightly from far off. The others shouted to him that he might as well forget trying to ride up the glass mountain, it could not be done. But the knight did not heed them; he galloped straight towards the glass mountain and rode up, even further than the knight in the copper armour. But when he had ridden perhaps two-thirds of the way up, he turned his horse around and rode down again. The King's daughter liked this knight even better, and sat there hoping that he would come all the way up. But when she saw him turning back, she threw her second golden apple after him, and it rolled down into his shoe. As soon as he was down from the hill, he rode away so quickly that nobody could see what had become of him.

That evening, when all the princes and knights were summoned to parade before the king and his daughter, so that the one with the golden apple could produce it and reveal his identity, one after another passed, but none of them had a golden apple. Like the day before, the brothers went home late in the evening and re-counted what had happened that day, how everyone had ridden, but nobody was able to make it up the hill.

"But after a long time a knight in a silver armour came along, and his horse had a silver bridle and a silver saddle," they said. "Now, *he* knew how to ride! He rode more than two-thirds of the way up the glass mountain, and then he turned back. He was really impressive! The princess threw him her second golden apple," the brothers said.

"Gosh, I would have liked to see *him* too," said Cinderlad.

"Right! He was a bit more shiny than the ashes you are poking around in, you ugly, dirty beast!" said the brothers.

On the third day everything happened just like the first two days: Cinderlad wanted to go with his brothers to watch the riding contest, but they refused to take him with them. And when they arrived at the glass hill, none of the contestants made it even a yard up the mountain. Everyone was waiting for the knight in the silver armour, but there was no sight or sound of him. But after a long time a man on a horse appeared, and they were such a marvellous sight that nobody there had ever seen anything like it. The knight wore a golden suit of armour, and his horse had a golden saddle and a golden bridle, and together they were so shiny and bright they glittered and gleamed and shone from far, far away. The other knights and princes did not even remember to call out it was not worth trying, for they were so overwhelmed by how resplendent he was. He galloped straight at the glass hill and flew up to the top so quickly that the princess did not even have time to hope that he would come all the way to the top. As soon as he reached the top, he snatched the third golden apple from the princess's lap, turned his horse around and rode back down again. And then he too disappeared from their sight before they knew what had happened.

When the two brothers returned home that evening, they held forth about what had happened at the riding contest that day, and finally they also told about the knight in the golden armour.

"He was really amazing, that man! There is no other knight to match him in all the world," said the brothers.

"Gosh, I would have liked to see *him*, me too," said Cinderlad.

"Yes, it does not glow that well in the heap of ashes you lie in, you dirty beast!" said the brothers.

The next day all the knights and princes were to parade before the King and the princess – I suppose it must have been too late the night before – for the contestant with the golden apple to make himself known. One after another they paraded, first the princes and then the knights, but none of them had the golden apple.

"Well, somebody must have it," said the king. "For we all saw with our own eyes that someone rode up the hill and took it." And so he ordered everyone in the kingdom to come to the manor and show the golden apple, if they had it. And so they came, one after another. But nobody had the golden apple. After a long time, Cinderlad's two brothers were also summoned to the manor. They were the last ones to appear before the King, and so the King asked if there was really no one else in the entire kingdom.

"Well, we do have a brother," they said. "But, *he* can't have taken the golden apple, for he didn't leave his pile of ashes on any of those days."

"Never mind that," said the King. "When everyone else has been to the manor, then he can come too." And so Cinderlad had to go to the manor house.

"Do you have the golden apple?" asked the King.

"Why, yes. Here is one, and here is the second one, and here is the third one too," said Cinderlad, as he pulled the three golden apples out of his pocket. Then he threw off his sooty rags and stood before them in his golden armour – gleaming and shining.

"Then you shall have my daughter and half my kingdom. You have earned both her and it," said the king.

A wedding was held, and Cinderlad married the princess. And there was much merrymaking at the wedding, you know, for they all knew how to make merry, even if they couldn't ride a horse up the glass hill. And if they haven't stopped their merrymaking yet, why, then they're probably still at it.

THE BOY
AND
THE DEVIL

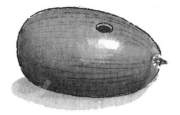

Once upon a time a boy was walking along a road cracking nuts. And as he came across a worm-eaten one, he met the Devil himself.

"Is it true what they say?" said the boy, "that you can make yourself as small as you wish and crawl through the eye of a needle?"

"Yes, I can," replied the Devil.

"Well, would you please show me, by crawling into this nut?" asked the boy.

And that's precisely what the Devil did.

No sooner had the Devil crawled through the worm-hole,

than the boy closed the hole with a twig.

"Now I've got you," he said, and put the nut in his pocket.

After a while the boy came to a forge, and he asked the blacksmith if he could crack the nut for him.

"That shouldn't be difficult," answered the blacksmith. And he took his smallest hammer, placed the nut on his anvil and struck it. But the nut wouldn't crack. So he tried with a bigger hammer, but not even that one was heavy enough. And then he tried an even bigger one, but that wouldn't crack the nut either.

By now the blacksmith was furious, and he grabbed his sledgehammer. "I'll crack you this time!" he said as he hit the nut with all his might. Then the nut burst into splinters, giving off such a roar that half the roof blew off and it seemed as though the whole smithy would come crashing down.

"I think the Devil himself was in that nut!" said the smith.

"He *was*," said the boy.

Hans Tinderstick
who made the
King's Daughter
laugh

Once upon a time there was a king who had a daughter so beautiful that she was famous far and wide. But she had such a serious nature that she was unable to laugh, and she put on such airs that she said no to all the suitors that came and asked for her hand. She didn't want to marry any of them, no matter how rich they were, whether they were princes or counts or dukes. The king had grown tired of this game long ago and wanted her to get married, just like everyone else. There was no reason to wait any longer, for she was old enough, and she was not getting any richer than she already was, for half the kingdom was to be hers – which was her inheritance from her mother.

So the king let it be known in the parish and far and wide that whoever could make his daughter laugh, would have her and half the kingdom. But anyone who tried and failed, would have three red strips out of his back and salt rubbed into the wounds. As you can imagine, there were many sore backs in the kingdom at that time. Suitors came from south and north and from east and west, thinking it must be the simplest thing in the world to make a princess laugh. And many quer men showed up to try their luck. But no matter how many monkeys and how many monkeyshines they made, the princess remained as gloomy and serious as ever.

Not far from the kings manor lived a man who had three sons. They had also heard the King's announcement that whoever could make his daughter laugh, would have her and half the kingdom.

The eldest brother wanted to try his luck first, so off he went. When he came to the manor, he said to the King that he wanted to have a go at making the princess laugh.

"That's all well and good," said the King, "but I doubt it will do you much good, young man, for so many men have tried before you. My daughter is so melancholy that I don't think there's much point in you even trying, and I don't want to see any more people coming to harm."

But the lad thought it was worth trying. It couldn't be so difficult for *him* to make a princess laugh, for he had made so many people laugh before, both gentlefolk and peasants, when he served as a soldier and mimicked the captains and generals. He went into the courtyard outside the princess's window and started impersonating all the various captains and generals. But it was of no use. The princess remained as straight-faced and serious as ever. So they took him and cut three broad red strips out of his back and sent him home.

Once he was back home, the second son wanted to try his luck. He was a schoolmaster and a rather strangelooking chap. He limped because his one leg was much longer than the other. One minute he looked as short as a child, and the next he stood up on his long leg, and was as tall as a troll. He was also rather a storyteller.

So off he went to the manor and said he wanted to try making the King's daughter laugh. Now, this one might have a chance, thought the King, "but may God comfort you if you fail," he said. "We are carving the strips wider for each person who tries and fails."

The schoolmaster rushed into the courtyard and took his position outside the princess' window. He preached and recited incantations in the style of seven well-known priests, and he read and sang in the style of seven well-known choristers who had served in the parish. The King laughed so hard he had to lean on a pillar to hold himself up, and even the princess showed the beginnings of a small smile, but then she became as straight-faced and serious as ever again. And so Paul the schoolmaster fared no better than Per the soldier, for surely

you know that their names were Per and Paul. They took him and cut three broad red strips out of his back and rubbed salt in the wounds, and then sent him back home.

Now the youngest son wanted to have a go, and his name was Hans Tinderstick. His brothers laughed at him and mocked him and showed him their sore backs, and their father did not want to let him go, for, he said, there couldn't be of any use for *him* to try who had no wit. He didn't know anything and didn't do anything but sit in the fireplace like a cat, poking around in the ashes and making tindersticks. But Hans Tinderstick did not give up. He begged and pleaded so persistently that in the end they grew tired of his nagging and let him go to the manor to try his luck.

When he arrived at the manor, he didn't say he wanted to try to make the King's daughter laugh; instead he asked for work. No, there was no work for him, they said, but Hans Tinderstick did not give up. Perhaps they could use someone to carry wood and water for the cook and the kitchen maids in such a large palace, he said. Yes, the King found that a good idea, and besides, I suppose he had had enough of his nagging. So, in the end, Hans Tinderstick was allowed to stay there and carry wood and water for the cook and the kitchen maids.

One day when fetching water from the stream, he saw a large fish hiding under an old pine root from which the water had washed the earth away. He slipped his bucket very slowly under the fish. As he was on his way back home to the palace, he met an old woman leading a golden goose.

"Good morning, grandmother!" said Hans Tinderstick. "What a beautiful bird, and such splendid feathers! They glitter and gleam from miles away. With feathers like that, a lad wouldn't have to make tindersticks."

The old woman liked the look of the fish that Hans had in his bucket better and said he could have the golden goose if he gave her the fish. The thing about the goose was that anyone who touched it, would be stuck, if you said: *Why don't you join us?*

This sounded like a good exchange to Hans Tinderstick. "A bird is better than a fish," he said to himself. "If what you say is true, I can use it as a fishing hook," he said to the old woman and was very happy with his goose.

He had not walked far before he met an old woman. When she saw the splendid golden goose, her fingers itched to touch it. She put on her sweetest look and her prettiest voice, and asked Hans if she could please pet his handsome golden goose.

"Why, of course you can!" said Hans Tinderstick, "but don't pull any feathers out!"

As soon as she touched the bird, he said: *Why don't you join us?* The old woman pulled and struggled to get free, but she was stuck to the goose and had to join them, whether she liked it or not, and Hans Tinderstick carried on as if he were alone with his golden goose.

266

When he had walked a little way further, he met a man who had some unfinished business with the old woman regarding a trick she had played on him. When he saw that she was struggling so hard to break free and understood that she was stuck, he found it safe to give her a reward to show her he hadn't forgotten, and so he gave her a good kick with one foot.

Why don't you join us? said Hans Tinderstick, and the man had to follow them, hopping along on one leg, whether he wanted to or not. The more he struggled and pulled and tried to get free, the worse it became, for then he was about to fall backwards.

Now they walked a fair distance almost to the manor house where they met the King's blacksmith; he was on his way to the forge and was carrying a large pair of blacksmith's tongs. Now, the blacksmith was a bit of a prankster and was always full of mischief and trouble, and when he saw the party approaching, hopping and stumbling along, he laughed so hard he bent over double, but then he said:

"This must be a new flock of geese for the princess. I wonder which of them is the gander and which is the goose? I suppose that chap waddling along in front must be the gander. Here goosy, goosy, goosy!" he called and waved his arm around as if he was scattering seed for the geese.

But the flock did not stop – the old woman and the man sim-

ply scowled at the smith because he was making fun of them. Then the smith said: "It might be fun to hold up the whole flock all at once." For he was a strong man, and he took hold of the old man's behind with his tongs, and the man shouted and struggled, but Hans Tinderstick said: *Why don't you join us?*

And so the blacksmith had to join them too. He arched his back, dug his feet into the ground and tried to pull free. But it was of no use, he was as firmly stuck to the flock as if he were screwed into the large vice in the forge, and whether he wanted to or not, he had to join the merry dance.

As they approached the palace, the guard dog came running up to them and started barking and yapping as if they were a pack of wolves or trolls, and when the King's daughter looked

out of her window to see what all the fuss was about and caught sight of the motley crew, she started to laugh. But Hans Tinderstick was not satisfied yet.

"Wait a moment and she'll really split her sides!" he said and disappeared behind the palace with his procession.

As they passed the kitchen, the door was open and the cook was stirring the porridge. When she saw Hans Tinderstick and

his flock, she ran out of the door with a stirring-stick in one hand and a ladle full of steaming porridge in the other, fit to burst with laughter. When she saw the blacksmith in the party, she slapped her thigh and started howling with laughter. Once she had finished laughing, *she* too found the golden goose so beautiful that she simply had to pet it.

"Hans, Hans!" she shouted, running after him with the ladle in her hand. "May I stroke your pretty bird?"

"Why don't you stroke me instead!" said the blacksmith.

"Why of course you can!" said Hans the Tinderstick Boy.

But when the cook heard what the blacksmith said, she became furious. "What did you say?" she shrieked and walloped the blacksmith with her ladle.

Why don't you join us? said Hans at that moment, and so she was stuck as well. And no matter how she swore and how she pulled and struggled and how wild she was, she had to hop along with the rest of them.

When they passed outside the princess' window, she was waiting for them, and when she saw that the cook had joined the procession too, with her ladle and stirring-stick, she roared with laughter and laughed so hard that the King had to hold her up.

And so Hans Tinderstick got the princess and half the kingdom, and there was a wedding that was heard and talked about throughout the kingdom.

THE SEVEN
FOALS

Once upon a time, there was a couple who was very poor. They lived in a miserable little cottage deep in the forest, from hand to mouth, and even that was hard enough. But they had three sons, and the youngest of them was called Cinderlad, for he did nothing but poking around in the ashes all day.

One day the eldest boy said he would go off to earn a living, to which his parents agreed at once. And he set off into the world. He walked and he walked all day long, and when it drew towards evening, he came to a royal manor house. The king was standing outside on the steps and asked him where he was off.

"Oh, I'm just wandering around looking for work, Sir," said
the boy.

"Would you like to work for me and look after my seven
foals?" asked the King. "If you can watch them for a whole day
and in the evening tell me what they eat and drink, you shall
have the princess and half my kingdom. But if you can't, I will
cut three red strips out of your back."

Well, the boy thought this sounded like an easy job and was
sure he would be able to do it.

In the morning, when the sun rose, the head groom let out
the seven foals. They ran off, with the boy following them, and
I'm sure they ran over hill and dale, through bushes and scrub.
After the boy had been running like this for a good while, he
began to be tired, and after another good while, he had had
enough of the whole foal-watching. All at once he came to a
small cave in the rock face, and sitting in the mouth of the
cave was an old woman spinning on a spindle. When she
caught sight of the boy running behind the foals, the sweat
pouring off him, the old woman called out:
"Come here, come here, my handsome son, and I shall pick
the lice off you!"

Now, the boy thought this sounded like a good idea, and he sat
in the cave with the old woman and laid his head in her lap. She
spent the whole day picking lice off him, while he lay there lazily.

When evening drew near, the boy wanted to leave.

"I suppose I might as well go straight home again," he said. "For there is no point in me going back to the King's manor now."

"Wait a little until dusk," said the old woman. "Then the King's foals will pass by here again. You can run home with them and nobody will ever know that you spent the whole day lying here instead of watching the foals."

When the foals came along, she gave the boy a jug of water and a piece of moss. He was to show them to the King and say that *this* is what the seven foals ate and drank.

"Did you watch my foals faithfully and well all day long?" the King asked when the boy came before him that evening.

"Yes, so I did," said the boy.

"Then I suppose you are able to tell me what my seven foals eat and drink?" asked the king.

The boy showed him the water jug and the moss the old woman had given him. "This is what they eat, and this is what they drink," said the boy.

Then the king understood how the lad had watched his foals, and became so angry he ordered them to chase the boy from the place immediately. But first they were to cut three red strips out of his back and rub salt into the wounds.

You can imagine in what kind of mood the boy was when he

arrived back home. He had gone out once to find work, he said, but he would never do it again.

The following day the second son said he wanted to go out into the world and try his luck. His parents said no and suggested he'd look at his brother's back. But he would not give up, he stuck to his plan, and eventually his parents let him go, and off he went. When he had walked the whole day, he too arrived at the royal manor house and found the King standing ouside on the steps. The king asked where he was bound. And when the boy replied that he was looking for work, the king said he could serve at his manor and watch his seven foals. The king set the same punishment and the same reward for him as he had set for his brother. The lad accepted immediately and entered into the king's service, for he would be able enough to watch the foals and tell the king what they ate and drank, he claimed.

At the crack of dawn the head groom let the seven foals out. Off they went, over hill and dale, and the boy ran after them. But the same thing happened to him as his brother: When he had been running behind the foals for a long, long time, so long that he was both sweaty and tired, he passed a cave. At the mouth of the cave sat an old woman spinning on a spindle, and she called out to the boy:
"Come here, come here, my handsome son, and I shall pick the lice off you!"

The boy thought this sounded like a nice idea, and he left the foals to run on wherever they pleased and sat down in the cave with the old woman. And there he sat and there he lay and there he did nothing the whole day long.

When the foals came back in the evening, the old woman gave him a piece of moss and a jug of water and told him to show them to the king. But when the king asked the lad: "Can you tell me what my seven foals eat and drink?" and the boy pulled out the clump of moss and the jug of water and said: "Yes, this is what they eat and this is what they drink," the king grew very angry and ordered them to cut three red strips out of his back, rub salt in them and chase him away on the spot. When he got back home, he too told them what had befallen him and said that he had gone out to look for work once, but that he would never do it again, that was for sure.

On the third day Cinderlad wanted to set out to make his fortune. He wouldn't mind trying to watch the king's seven foals, he said.

The others laughed at him and made fun of him.

"You've seen what happened to us, but you think *you* can succeed. That's likely, you who never did anything but poking around in the ashes!" they said.

"Yes, but I want to anyway, I do," said Cinderlad. "For I have made up my mind." And no matter how much his brothers mocked and how much his parents begged, they couldn't make him change his mind, and so Cinderlad set off.

After he had walked all day, he arrived at the kings' manor house at dusk. The king was standing outside on the steps and asked where he was bound.

"I'm out and about looking for work," said Cinderlad.

"Where are you from?" the king asked, for he wanted to know a little bit more now before he took anyone into his service.

Cinderlad told him where he was from and said he was the brother of the other two who had watched the king's seven foals. And then he asked if *he* might also try to watch them the next day.

"Shame on them!" said the king and flew into a rage at the very memory of them. "If you are the brother of those two lay-abouts, you can't be of much use either. I've had enough of your sort!"

"Yes, but since I'm already here, I might as well be allowed to try, also?" said Cinderlad.

"Well, if you're so keen to have your back flayed, it's fine by me," said the king.

"I'd much rather have the princess," said Cinderlad.

At the first light of dawn the head groom let the seven foals out, and off they ran over hill and dale, through bushes and scrub, with Cinderlad following close behind.

When he had been running like this for a long while, he too

came to the cave. The old woman was sitting there again, spinning on her spindle. She called out to Cinderlad: "Come here, come here, my handsome son, and I shall pick the lice off you!"

"Kiss my arse, you old hag! Kiss my arse!" Cinderlad replied, leaping and running and holding on to the tail of one of the foals.

When they were well past the cave, the youngest foal said: "Why don't you jump up on to my back, for we still have a long way to go." And Cinderlad did so.

They travelled a long, long way and then a bit further. "Can you see anything yet?" said the foal.

"No," said Cinderlad.

So they travelled a good way farther.

"Can you see anything yet?" asked the foal.

"No," said the boy.

When they had travelled a long, long way again, the foal asked again: "Can you see anything yet?"

"Yes, I think I can see something white," said Cinderlad. "It looks like a huge, enormous birch stump."

"Good, we're going in there," said the foal.

When they finally came to the birch stump, the eldest foal broke it aside. There was a door where the stump had been, and inside the door was a tiny room not containing much more than a small fireplace and a couple of stools. But behind the door hung a large, rusty sword and a small jug.

"Can you brandish the sword?" asked the foal.

Cinderlad tried, but he couldn't. In that case, he would have to drink a drop from the jug. He took one swig, then another, and then a third, and then he could brandish it just like that.

"Now you must take the sword with you," said the foal. "With it you shall chop off all our heads on your wedding day, and then we will become princes again, like we were before. For we are the brothers of the princess you will have when you can tell the king what we eat and drink. A terrible troll cast a spell on us. Once you have chopped our heads off, you must take care to put each head next to the tail of the body it belongs to, and then the troll's curse will have no more power over us."

Cinderlad promised to do this, and then they pushed onwards.

When they had travelled a long, long way, the foal asked: "Can you see anything?"

"No," said Cinderlad.

So they travelled a good way further. "And now?" asked the foal. "Can you see anything now?"

"No, nothing," said Cinderlad.

Then they travelled many, many miles farther, over many hills and dales.

"What about now?" said the foal. "Can't you see anything yet?"

"Yes, I can," said Cinderlad. "I can see what looks like a kind of blue stripe a long, long way off."

"Good, that's a river," said the foal, "and we are to cross it."

There was a long, fine bridge over the river, and when they reached the other side, they travelled onwards again a long, long way. The foal asked Cinderlad again if he could see any-thing.

Yes, this time he could see something black on the horizon that looked a bit like a church spire.

"Good, we're going to go in there," said the foal.

As soon as the foals entered the churchyard, they turned into young men looking like princes, their clothes so splendid they seemed to shine. They went inside the church, and the priest behind the altar gave them bread and wine. Cinderlad went in too. Once the priest had laid his hands upon the prin-ces and blessed them, they went out of the church again. So did Cinderlad, he brought with him a bottle of wine and a pie-ce of altar bread. As soon as the seven princes stepped out into the churchyard, they turned into foals again. Cinderlad jumped on to the back of the youngest foal, and they set off on the way they had come, but this time they travelled much, much faster. First they crossed the bridge, then they passed the birch stump, and then they went past the old woman spinning in her cave. They were moving so quickly that Cinderlad couldn't hear what the old woman shrieked at him, but enough to know that she was in a furious rage.

It was almost dark when they arrived back at the manor house that evening, and the King himself was standing in the courtyard waiting for them.

"Did you watch my foals faithfully and well all day long?" the King asked Cinderlad.

"I did my best," said Cinderlad.

"Then I suppose you are able to tell me what my seven foals eat and drink, aren't you?" said the king.

Cinderlad brought out the altar bread and the bottle of wine and showed them to the king.

"This is what they eat, and this is what they drink," he said.

"Indeed, you watched my foals faithfully and well," said the King, "and you shall have the princess and half my kingdom."

Then they made preparations for the wedding, and it would

be so grand and regal that it would be heard and talked about far and wide, said the King.

While they were sitting at the wedding banquet, the bridegroom rose and went down to the stables, for he had forgotten something there that he had to fetch, he said. When he reached the stables, he did as the foals had said and chopped off all of their heads. He started with the eldest, and then chopped the heads off all the others according to age, and took great care to lay each head by the tail of the foal it had belonged to. And as soon as he did it, they turned back into princes.

When he entered the wedding banquet with the seven princes, the king was so happy that he both kissed and hugged Cinderlad, and his bride grew even fonder of him than she had been before.

"You already have half the kingdom," said the king, "and now you shall have the other half when I die, for my sons will be able to get countries and kingdoms of their own now they are princes again."

There was much rejoicing and merrymaking at that wedding, don't you know.

I was there too, but everybody was too busy to notice me. All I got was a piece of cake with butter on it. I put the cake on the oven, and the cake burned and the butter ran, and in the end I didn't get so much as a crumb.